ANDY MCILREE

Grace in First Peter

The Many Splendoured Grace Revealed to an
Ungracious Man

✝ HAYES PRESS

Second edition

This book was professionally typeset on Reedsy.
Find out more at reedsy.com

Contents

1. GRACE REQUIRED IN AN UNGRACIOUS MAN

It's unlikely that you have ever received a letter without your first question being, "Who is it from?" It should be the same when we begin to read the letters in the New Testament of our Bibles. We really ought to know who the penman is behind the writing. We know, of course, that it has come from God, but behind each one is a man whom God shaped for the purpose. Peter, who has been called 'the big fisherman,' was an unlikely candidate for letter writing. If he had been told, while hauling in his nets, that he would write letters some day, he probably would have said, "In your dreams!"

As we start to think of him, we need to link him with others who were given the same privilege. Paul's letters, for instance, cause us to realise the kind of company that Peter knew he was in, yet there's no hiding that he had the advantage of walking with the Lord throughout the days of His ministry, of being at Calvary to see the way his Saviour died, and of meeting Him in resurrection. Paul missed all that, but was compensated in other ways during the three years following his conversion, as we read in Galatians 1:11-18.

Tracing the grace of God in Peter's first letter is like seeing the glory of God in Romans and the greatness of God in Hebrews, but this doesn't suggest at all that these other letters don't have what Peter has in his. When we think of the glory of God in Romans, we are very much aware that His glory is associated with His greatness and grace. Likewise, when we step into Hebrews to consider the greatness of God, we soon realise that it expresses His glory and grace; and now, as we focus on the grace of God in Peter's five chapters, we become just as conscious that it is seen in His glory and greatness. Taking these altogether, we rejoice that each one is expressed in Christ, and this is the beauty of studying them.

It was vital before Peter dipped his pen into the ink that God would reveal much to him as he drank deeply from the wells of salvation. God was about to use him to speak to others, so firstly He must speak to him. Let's not deceive ourselves; we will never be able to speak to others about our Lord Jesus Christ unless the Spirit of God has fulfilled His ministry by speaking first to us about Him. As Peter took up his pen and thought of how far-flung his readers were, he must have felt it strange for a man who hardly knew the outside of a boat, yet this was the plan God had in mind when he called him. When the Saviour paused on the beach to call him and Andrew from the fishing boat (1), he had no idea of what lay ahead. Their stepping out reflected Abram's faith and obedience as he *"went out, not knowing where he was going"* (2); and *"the Lord of glory"* (3) appeared to them just as *"the God of glory"* (4) appeared to him.

Peter was probably within earshot when Jesus told the Pharisees, *"Your father Abraham rejoiced to see My day, and he saw it and was glad"* (5). What a contrast, that they saw Him up close and rejected Him! Abraham was unusual for he knew more about predestination than he knew about destination. Years later, it was very different for Ruth as she left Moab. She knew that she was going to Bethlehem, but had no idea that she was destined for Matthew 1:5 to be a vital link in the royal line that led to the Lord Jesus. She was the opposite of Abraham for she knew about her destination, but didn't have the slightest clue about predestination.

As for Peter, God in His wisdom had a plan for him, which included writing two letters that would find their way into His written Word to sit side by side, and in absolute agreement, with the writings of Paul; but before we read any more from his letter we need to explore the first word:

Peter

Paul and Peter had a major disagreement, yet two points should be clarified right away. Yes, they had a dispute, of which Paul wrote, *"I withstood him to his face"* (6). No, it didn't mean that this led to a divergence in their beliefs and teaching. These two men had been at loggerheads with each other, and there was good reason why they had stood toe to toe, face to face, and eye to eye, for Paul recognised that Peter had compromised himself before God and before Gentile believers.

Peter had heard that men were coming from James, and he panicked. He took fright, because he had been saying things among the Gentiles that he shouldn't have said. It wasn't simply that he was eating with them, he had made adjustments to the gospel for them, but when he heard these men were coming he *"withdrew and separated himself"* (7). He put them out of sight and distanced himself from them, as if they never existed. In his mind, they were gone. He had shunned them and completely shut them out, so that he excluded and no longer countenanced them.

He had gone into reverse mode, which Paul called *"hypocrisy"* (8) and *"withstood him to his face"* (9) for the problem was doctrinal and serious. Peter's compromise had misrepresented the truth of the gospel and was so influential that it misled Barnabas. Paul wouldn't tolerate this and confronted Peter in a way that could be translated as "he opposed him and faced him down." Weakness would have stepped back, but with appropriate spiritual strength Paul stepped up to the challenge. It may sound as though Paul was being ungracious, yet it's even more direct in the Greek language, which says, *"kata prosōpon"* – he faced him down. Yes, he was gracious enough to tell his brother that he was a hypocrite, which was hardly the qualification for a man of God, an apostle, for a disciple or a writer.

Their dispute didn't last, for both of them knew that they had such an affinity with each other that caused them to be mightily used of God, since they knew that the Spirit of God was at work in each other's ministry, resulting in an overlap in what they taught. These dear men were not out of synchrony. An indication of harmony in what they communicated is seen in Galatians 2:8, where Paul summed up the harmony of their commission by saying, *"For He who worked effectively in Peter for the apostleship to the circumcised also worked effectively in me toward the Gentiles."* This is a tremendous acknowledgement from Paul and it confirms:

- **Harmony of calling** - Their call from God as apostles
- **Harmony in commission** - Their ministry was according to the mind of the Holy Spirit
- **Harmony in communication** - Their teaching corresponded

Peter reciprocated Paul's genuine, and generous, acknowledgement of his ministry by adding, *"consider that the longsuffering of our Lord is salvation—as also our beloved brother Paul, according to the wisdom given to him, has written to you, as also in all his epistles, speaking in them of these things, in which are some things hard to understand, which untaught and unstable people twist to their own destruction, as they do also the rest of the Scriptures"* (10). If there had been any lingering doubt or discomfort in Peter's mind, he could easily have re-phrased this to 'your beloved brother Paul,' and not everyone would have noticed his evasion. Instead, he thought of the brother who faced him down, looked him in the eye and told him that he was a hypocrite, and called him *"beloved."* That took grace!

Perhaps we should pause here to listen to Peter the fisherman talking about the *"Hebrew of the Hebrews"* (11) and learn how God takes up servants from different backgrounds and ability to produce their mutual regard for one another. John and Peter shared the same upbringing and occupation in Galilee and were described as *"uneducated and untrained,"* (12) which meant their schooling wasn't from rabbis and that they were mere layman whose confidence and plain speaking came from being in Jesus' company. Peter thought highly of Paul's delight and reasoning in the Old Testament Scriptures, but Peter must have done this too. Would God not have us assume that, since Simon was the one to whom Andrew made a beeline when he *"found the Messiah,"* (13) that he was among those who were *"waiting for the Consolation of Israel"* (14)?

At the time of his calling, Simon may have been less academic than Saul of Tarsus, but more devout. In his on-going devotion, he had an appreciation of divine things revealed through Paul that were *"hard to understand,"* things that others would twist. He knew there were twisters around, and so did other writers like Paul, John, James and Jude (15). Even so, it's not only that he ascribes high regard for Paul's spiritual ability. He goes much farther by recognising that Paul's writings form part of Scripture, which is clearly implied in his condemnation of those who perverted his reasoning – Gr. *hōs kai tas loipas graphas* – *"as they do also the rest of the Scriptures"* (16). What a marvellous acknowledgement that Paul's letters are equated with the other Scriptures!

Some readers may be inclined to respond to him by saying, 'Hold on Peter, do you know what you are saying?' and his reply would be, 'Yes, of course I know! He is my *"beloved brother"* and I am speaking of *"all his epistles."* I love the man, I laud his ministry; and, above all, I have learned that his letters are part of the sacred Scriptures.' In saying, *"as they do also the rest of the Scriptures,"* he linked them with other Old Testament writings as the revealed Word of God. How well he knew that what others twisted and bent out of shape was nothing less than the inspired Word of God.

Earlier, in 2 Peter 1:20-21, Peter confirmed that *"no prophecy of Scripture is of any private interpretation, for prophecy never came by the will of man, but men of God spoke as they were moved by the Holy Spirit."* This was his way of re-wording and expanding Paul's statement that *"All Scripture is given by inspiration of God"* (17) – Gr. *theopneustos* – meaning it is *"breathed out by God"* (17), thus acknowledging that Paul's letters are part of God's inspired and inerrant Word.

Wherever each New Testament letter went, to an individual church or groups of churches, it was shared with believers, and we might well ask, 'How did they take it in the first time they heard it?' It's much easier to conclude that these early Christians must have gathered many times to search out the teaching that God the Inspirer wanted them to enjoy. What a vital example for us: for if present-day believers are so busy that they have no time to fit in regular teaching of God's Word, then the truth is they are too busy; and their churches are dying, even if they also are busy! We need to beware of the Sardis syndrome: reputed to be lively, but dead (18).

As Peter thought on all that Paul had written, he must have had the longing that the grace of God would do the same through him; that he

6

also would be so beloved that the Inspirer would breathe out His Word through him. It's not that Paul and Peter wrote words and God breathed into them. He breathed out the words, and Peter's concern was that men were twisting God's out-breathed Word.

Sadly, what they did with the Old Testament, others do with the New. There is no end of theories that contradict sound theology and they come from twisters who by nature oppose the straightness of His truth. When God used the Hebrew word *torah* to describe His Old Testament law, He had its root meaning from the word *yarah* in mind, and nothing could be straighter for it depicts an archer shooting an arrow. He sends it on its course toward its target by the corresponding straightness of the Holy Spirit's work, while twisted minds attempt to deflect it by twisting what it means. Peter's earlier inconsistent behaviour didn't lead to his being numbered with untaught and unstable twisters, but Paul was used by God to correct him after he had been guilty of misapplying the gospel and misleading his Gentile hearers.

How thankful we can be that God spoke so openly about disagreements between His workers and didn't ignore them or sweep them under the carpet. Differences of opinion aren't hard to find in the Bible, but it's wonderful to see how He helped divided minds get back together again, whether it happened in the Old Testament or in the New. Our minds go back to a much earlier dispute between Moses and Aaron. There's a great lesson in how Moses handled the problem in Deuteronomy chapter 9, especially when he came to verse 20, where he said, *"so I prayed for Aaron also at the same time."* What a great attitude!

God's openness about all these matters shows that He provides the way to put things right. It's not wrong to disagree, but reaching agreement has to be done His way. I started off by talking about Moses and Aaron, and I'll finish by going back to another example of Moses' ability to help him. It's in Leviticus 10 and, once again, he was really concerned about a mistake Aaron had made. The good thing is, that having shown him how troubled he was about it, he then let him explain himself, and the chapter ends by saying, *"So when Moses heard that, he was content"* (19). It was a great way to round off a disagreement about how the Lord should be served, and our prayer is that what we have been talking about with you will end in exactly the same way.

In Psalm 45, David wrote, *"My tongue is the pen of a ready writer."* Peter could talk, and we will think later of how saying the wrong things landed him in trouble. He was a talker. There were men in the Old Testament called Amorites, and the word *'amar* includes the thought that they were talkers. When David thought about the ministry of the Holy Spirit through him he said, *"The Spirit of the LORD spoke by me, and His word was on my tongue"* (20). This is where Peter wanted to be, if he ever was going to be among God's writers, and he could have said, *"For there is not a word on my tongue, but behold, O LORD, You know it altogether"* (21). There were things that he had said to the Lord Jesus Christ that were wrong.

We are thinking of grace that was required by an ungracious man for that's what Peter was. It's also what we were and, to some extent, still are. We are perfectly capable of saying something out of place. As we read through the five chapters of this letter, we will discover that this man is in harmony, not only with Paul but also with the Inspirer. He is moved by the Inspirer and assures us that no prophecy of scripture is *"of private interpretation, for ... men of God spoke as they were moved by the Holy Spirit."*

Paul had summed this up in a word – *theopneustos* – but the fisherman's mind wanted to know the practical outworking of its meaning. No one else in the Bible ever used Paul's word, so perhaps it was an academic's appreciation, whereas Peter wanted to describe how the word worked by telling us that *"men of God spoke as they were moved by the Holy Spirit."* They were carried along by His divine presence and power. That is, they were carried by the Holy Spirit from where they were to where God wanted them to be, since they were incapable of carrying themselves.

Let's ask ourselves if we are living in the enjoyment of being carried along by the Holy Spirit. We are not going to be inspired, but we have the inspired Word to share and we need to be carried along by Him. There are wrong ways to handle the Word of God. We can speak ungraciously (22). We can speak unadvisedly (23). We also can speak wickedly for God (24) by misrepresenting what He says and means. We should mean what we say by saying what He means, and not resort to false notions to support what we think He means! We can defend things we think we see in the Word that are not there at all, and end up speaking ungraciously, unadvisedly, and unrighteously for God.

As Peter began his letter, he was waiting for the Inspirer to breathe out His spoken Word as He had done with Paul. All we need to do is step into the first chapter and we will think we are in Romans 8. Note how he showed this in the way his first chapter mirrors it by emphasising its well-constructed gospel themes. Listen to him and trace the similarity as he echoes the great truths of:

- verse 2: election and foreknowledge - Romans 8:29
- verse 3: hope - Romans 8:24
- verse 3: resurrection - Romans 8:11
- verse 4: inheritance - Romans 8:17
- verses 5,9: predestination - Romans 8:29-30

- verse 7: glorification - Romans 8:30
- verse 15: called - Romans 8:30

All these are included in his masterly introduction and present a wonderfully coinciding overlap with all Paul has shared, and we catch the distinct sense that Peter has much more to develop. As his letter progressed, he introduced other aspects of truth that correspond with Paul's teaching in his letters. For example:

- Chapter 1: **Salvation**
- Chapter 2: **Service** – the house of God, and priestly service
- Chapter 3: **Submission** – compassion, and sanctification
- Chapter 4: **Supply** – its glory, its grace, its gifts
- Chapter 5: **Shepherding** – the Elderhood, and the little flock

How good it is for us to see that the man, who on some occasions had been so out of step, by the time he dipped his pen in the inkwell was ready to open with the first word, "Peter." It's such a contrast from our habit of signing letters with our name as the last word. Paul adopted the same practice as Peter. In fact, in 2 Corinthians 10:1, Paul triples the reference to himself by saying, *"Now I, Paul, myself."* Was this the promotion of self? No, these were gracious men. The God of glory who worked through Paul in his letter to the Romans is the God of grace who worked through Peter as he wrote to Pontus, Galatia, Cappadocia, Asia, and Bithynia. By His help, we will see more evidence of this as we continue.

(1) Mk.1:16,17 (2) Heb.11:8 (3) 1 Cor.2:8 (4) Gen.12:1; Acts 7:2 (5) Jn 8:56 (6) Gal.2:11 (7) Gal.2:12 (8) Gal.2:13 (9) Gal.2:11 (10) 2 Pet.3:15,16 (11) Phil.3:5 (12) Acts 4:13 (13) Jn 1:41,42 (14) Lk.2:25 (15) 1 Cor.11:19; 2 Cor.11:26; Gal.2:4; 1 Jn 4:1; Jas.1:26; Jude v.4 (16) 2 Pet.3:16 (17) 2

Tim.3:16, ESV (18) Rev.3:1 (19) Lev.10:20 (20) 2 Sam.23:2 (21) Ps.139:4 (22) Col.4:6 (23) Ps.106:33 (24) Job 13:7

1 Peter 1:1 & Luke 22:31-32

"*Peter, an apostle of Jesus Christ, to the pilgrims of the Dispersion in Pontus, Galatia, Cappadocia, Asia, and Bithynia ...*" (1 Peter 1:1).

"*And the Lord said, Simon, Simon! Indeed, Satan asked for you, that he may sift you as wheat. But I have prayed for you, that your faith should not fail; and when you have returned to Me, strengthen your brethren*" (Luke 22:31,32).

2. GRACE RESTORED IN HIS MISTAKES

Many thoughts probably went through Peter's mind as, in the wisdom of God, he began his letter by writing his name to introduce himself to those who may never have met him in their far-off new homeland now known as Turkey, far from where he had grown up in Galilee. We have thought of the grace that was required by an ungracious man, and can imagine his mixed feelings as he joyfully began to represent the Inspirer while sadly recalling how he disappointed his Saviour. As we consider the ups and downs of his life that lie between the lines of the opening verse, we can only begin to gauge what it meant to him when God asked him to write, like Paul, as an ambassador on *"Christ's behalf"* (1).

Thirty years had passed before the Lord Jesus Christ had gone from Bethlehem, the house of bread, via Egypt to Nazareth (2), then on to Bethsaida, the house of fishing, the birthplace of Simon and Andrew. Walking on the beach near Capernaum where they were now living, He had called them from their boat, as they were actively *"casting a net"* (3). He was interested in what we would call 'busy men', for God never calls the idle. The call that came from the Man on the shore didn't reach Peter on a day off or on an off day! Peter was like Elisha who was called when his hands were firmly on the plow, just as Simon's were firmly on the net. He was fully engaged in his work, a fisherman through and through, hook, line and sinker, until Jesus called him to fish on the landward side of the beach. Like the others, he left men to find men.

His work was his life, yet he had the expectation that the Messiah was coming. The Messianic hope was in his heart, otherwise Andrew would not have run to tell a brother who wasn't interested. For Simon and Andrew, James and John, the Man on their beach was the fulfilment of Paul's message, *"the grace of God that brings salvation has appeared"* (4). *"Immediately"* they left all to walk with the One who ministered grace, not least into Simon's faults that he might make him into the kind of man who would minister to others, including us. God doesn't hide His failures. He restores them. There's something very stimulating and encouraging about God's making room in His Word to record Simon's mistakes, but it's been well said that 'the man who never made a mistake never made anything.' Simon made lots of them, but the Lord made a lot out of him, and in this we find the grace that helps us not to lose heart when we fail. Failing doesn't make us a failure!

None of these men paid any attention to the new Figure who walked on their beach at the beginning of His ministry; nor did they know that the grace of God had appeared until He spoke, and believing men stepped forward. There was a very different reaction at the end of His ministry in Gethsemane when He said, *"I am"*, and unbelieving men fell backward. Four men left their boats, their father, their family, their friends, and their inheritance to follow a Man through whom they would discover that a far greater inheritance lay ahead of them.

What did the hired servants think as sons left their father with the future of the work in the hands of servants instead of sons? They also turned their backs on the waves and billows of Galilee to follow Him until He faced the waves and billows of Golgotha. *"All Your waves and billows have gone over Me"* (5) could have been written of Him as He endured the spiritual storm of the middle cross. He also called them spiritually to engage in the different aspects of their fishing habits.

In Matthew 4:18, they were *casting* a net; in Mark 1:19, they were *mending* their nets; and in Luke 5:2, they were *washing* their nets, but these were as nothing to Luke 5:6 when their net was *breaking*. What they had been accustomed to on a daily basis found its spiritual counterpart as they walked with Him. Each was a foretaste of Peter's dependence on the Lord for the day came when, meeting Him after His resurrection, he *"cast himself into the sea"* (6). He did with himself what he had done with the nets. Later, when he wrote to the churches in Galatia (7), his message was in harmony with Paul's appeal *"to restore"* a sinning brother (8). The word Paul used would appeal to Peter for *katartizō* is identical to what fishermen did when *"mending"* their nets. Peter was learning that the net was no longer in his hand, but in his pen; and it must have meant a lot to him that Paul used the same analogy.

It appealed so much to him that he used it himself in 1 Peter 5:10 when longing that the God of all grace would *"perfect"* those in the assemblies – meaning that He would restore their fellowship as a fisherman repairs a broken net. They were doing for people what they had done at the end of a catch, when their nets were breaking under the strain and they had to reconnect the broken mesh. Paul and Peter are interested in the God who restores broken men. It's one feature of *"He who worked effectively in Peter ... also worked effectively in me."*

Through his work, others would experience the *bathing* (Gr. *louō*) that the Lord grants in salvation (9). This was their spiritual washing – a thorough cleansing, just like the nets in Luke 5:2. Peter would never forget the lesson he learned from the Lord in this chapter for he discovered that the Son of God is in control of both sides of the beach and of the boat, and he submitted himself to His control (10). He had once been quite emphatic when he resisted the Lord's command and sailed out of His will by saying, *"Master, we have toiled all night and caught nothing."* His initial reaction was to debate with the Lord, as if to say, "Let me tell You something – we did this for a living, we know the sea, and it's pointless."

Then came the turnaround – *"nevertheless* [Gr. *de*: but] *at Your word I will let down the net"* – He introduced the *"but"* that delivered him from the selfishness of self and caused him to speak in submissiveness to the mind of the Lord, and he sailed into His will. The opposite was seen in John 6:9 when Andrew said, "There is a lad here who has five barley loaves and two small fish." If only he had stopped there, but he didn't. He added, "but what are they among so many?" He spoiled it by introducing the word *"but"* that caused him to be delivered from the mind of the Lord, to speak according to self, and sail out of His will. Isn't that what we do, too? Peter started well by saying, "Master" (Gr. *epistatēs*: commander), but didn't let Him have the mastery until after voicing his own will. But then he learned:

- **Acceptance** of the Lord's will, in spite of personal logic
- **Awareness** of the Lord's sinlessness and his own sinfulness
- **Assurance** of the Lord's help in catching men

In the acknowledgement of his own sinfulness, he also recognised his personal limitation. Lessons can be learned, progress can be made, but imperfect man can't become perfect in his actions. This includes Peter. He was an apostle, but his impulsive nature led him into other contradictions. For example:

1. His Defiance

a. When the Lord Jesus was speaking to His disciples in Matthew 16 they were in the north of Israel, in the region of Caesarea Philippi, now called Banias, near the foot of Mount Hermon where a spring becomes the Banias River and one of the tributaries of the River Jordan. Significantly, He had just introduced, for the first time, the great truth of building His church (v.18); and then, also for the first time, spoke of His death and resurrection through which it would be made a reality. Peter was standing there, and we know the conversation that took place when the Lord asked, *"Who do men say that I, the Son of Man, am?"* (11).

The people evidently had thought of this and suggested John the Baptist, Elijah or Jeremiah; apparent compliments, but were they? Hardly! They had concluded that John had *"a demon"* (12); Elijah had been called the *"troubler of Israel"* (13); and it had been said of Jeremiah, *"This man does not seek the welfare of this people, but their harm"* (14). To make matters worse, they thought Jesus was a blasphemer (15). Peter was in no doubt that He is *"the Christ, the Son of the living God,"* in full agreement with the I AM's eternal name (16). The Lord was revealing the Deity of His Person, but with the Person of Deity He revealed the purpose of Deity – to be the Builder of His church, which Paul described as *"the church, which is his body"* (17).

Peter listened well, but when the Saviour changed the subject to His inevitable suffering, death and resurrection, it was too much for him. He reacted strongly and took Jesus aside – Gr. *proslambanō*, which implies he seized Him and took Him aside, as if saying, "Come over here" – and then began to rebuke Him saying, *"Far be it from You, Lord; this shall not happen to You!"* (18). It was as if Peter felt he could enlighten the Lord for this could be translated as, "God forbid it, Lord, this shall definitely not happen to You", which was directly in opposition to the divine plan, and another contradiction by Peter. He had made the mistake of saying "Master" in Luke 5:5 before counter-reasoning with the Commander's will. Now, he opposed His Lordship by combining *"Far be it"* and *"this shall never happen to You"* with *"Lord."*

By using the word *kurios* he implied that he was subject to the authority of his Controller, yet strongly resisted what He said. The Lord immediately sensed the Tempter's voice behind Peter's words and addressed him directly by saying, *"Get behind Me, Satan! You are an offense to Me, for you are not mindful of the things of God, but the things of men."* Through Peter, he attempted to sow the doubt that the way of the cross was avoidable. Yes, Peter made a mistake, but *"He who worked effectively in Peter"* would turn him around, even though other mistakes would follow.

b. In the next chapter (19) Peter, James, and John were with the Lord on the Mount of Transfiguration when Moses and Elijah appeared as the representatives of the Law and the Prophets, undoubtedly appearing to honour the much greater glory of the One who had come to fulfil them (20). Luke says, they *"appeared in glory and spoke of His decease"* (21). They were discussing His exodus. The exodus of the children of Israel was because of the Passover lamb and well known to both men; but this time they talked about the exodus of the Lamb. Luke is the only one who tells us that the three disciples slept until *"when they were fully awake, they saw His glory and the two men who stood with Him"* (22). It wasn't when they were half-asleep, and this reminds us of the miracle of changing water into wine at the wedding in Cana of Galilee when He *"manifested His glory"* in waterpots that had been filled *"to the brim"* (23) – not half-filled – and it's still the same in our lives. It's not half-filled vessels that give Him glory, just as it wasn't the half-awake who saw His glory on the Mount.

Peter was fully awake to that glory, but it was a drowsy mind that wanted to let the Lord know what he was thinking. Once again, he began by saying, *"Master"* – still holding on to *epistatēs*, the Controller (i.e. more than Instructor, Commander), but denying its meaning. Then he added, *"it is good for us to be here"* – when he had been asleep for most of the time! To top it off, he went on to suggest, *"let us make three tabernacles, one for You, one for Moses, and one for Elijah"* (24). No wonder the voice of the Inspirer caused Luke to sum up Peter's mistake by concluding, *"not knowing* [Gr. *eidō:* as in perception, seeing] *what he said"* – that is, he had no idea. However, it would have been a greater mistake had he asked for six!

The day will come when Old Testament saints will share in His millennial glory (25), but the Mount was the revelation of the Saviour's supreme glory, and they were to *"Hear Him!"* and see *"Jesus only"* (26). The grace of God had appeared to them on the beach as the lowly Servant calling servants. On the Mount, the grace of God appeared again, this time in glory bringing sons to glory.

This was another of Peter's mistakes, but *"He who worked effectively in Peter"* was still working. Peter was an unfinished and on-going work, and so are we. God was working in him to produce a man who was fit to write for Him, just as He is still working in us to produce men and women who are fit to work for Him. Peter's letters show how well God turned him around for, in the first he tells us that he was *"a witness of the sufferings of Christ"* (27); and in the second he says, we *"were eyewitnesses of His majesty"* (28). He had become "fully awake" in every sense. We can be too, though our minds can switch off while we consider His Word, but it's when the mind is fully awake that it can absorb the richness of its ministry and we see the Saviour in ways that are manifestations of His glory.

2. His Defence

Peter leapt to the Lord's defence in the Garden of Gethsemane, even as the power of the *"I AM"* was unleashed and *"they drew back and fell to the ground"* (29). Imagine if He had spoken like this all the time. He could have done, but didn't. He could have unleashed the same force before Pilate when He spoke at Gabbatha, and sent him toppling from his judgment seat. He upholds *"all things by the word of His power"* (30), and He floored these people by it in Gethsemane. All too suddenly, the man who had stood in defiance, now felt he should stand in defence, and in a flash, his sword was drawn and off came Malchus' ear. Had Peter been a swordsman and not a fisherman, it could have been worse!

The Lord of Hosts could have called for *"more than twelve legions of angels"* (31), so there was no need for one of twelve disciples on earth to think he was needed for such a role. Earlier, as He prayed, one angel strengthened Him in Gethsemane (32); and there were only two who sat in the tomb where His body had lain (33). There was no need for hosts to accompany Him in His suffering, but they will come in His glory (34). In the Garden, Jehovah Sabaoth's voice was enough! And, once again, *"He who worked effectively in Peter"* brought him through this crisis too.

3. His Denial

The Lord anticipated Peter's denial (35), addressing him as, *"Simon, Simon."* Why not, "Peter"? Perhaps it was to indicate that the disciple was about to enter into something that was contrary to his new name (36), and out of character with his true spiritual walk. The Lord told him, *"Satan has asked to have you* [plural – all the disciples] *... But I have prayed for you"* (singular – meaning Simon in particular).

The old farming process of sifting was slow and laborious, either by tossing the grain upward into the wind and causing the chaff to separate from the wheat as it fell or by holding a riddle as high as possible, shaking it and, again, letting the wind blow away the chaff as the grain fell on to the threshing floor. The devil aimed to do the opposite for he always wants the grain to blow away, leaving only the chaff behind; so the Lord was insinuating, "Simon, Simon, Satan has asked to have you ... that he might make your life chaff ... but I have prayed for you."

He had been a complete outsider standing at the high priest's door until John asked the doorkeeper girl to let him in (37). Recognised and humiliated by her, he was brought to denial number one. Moving inside to warm himself at the fire, he was brought to denial number two by *"another girl"* (38) who shared her allegation with others that he had been with Jesus. Shortly afterwards, some bystanders approached him to say that they were sure of who he was, and denial number three hit home as the rooster crowed (39). Among them was *"one of the servants of the high priest, a relative of him whose ear Peter cut off"* (40). He had seen him in the lantern-light of Gethsemane, where the sword-wielder would have stood against all-comers, yet his predicted fall came at the word of two girls, some bystanders and a servant.

His denials were heard by all, and by the Lord who could have said, like Elisha who told Gehazi, *"Did not my heart go with you?"* (41). John tells us, *"He knew all men"* and *"what was in man"* (42) yet Peter said, *"I do not know Him."* Oh Peter, how could you say such a thing? Then we realise that in these hearts of ours there's the possibility of the same thing happening, even in the times when fear makes us hold back from witnessing. Fears, like faults, are the enemies of faith!

The devil wanted to make all their lives unfruitful, leaving no harvest for the Sower, and it's still his destructive plan for all believers; but how blessedly the Advocate prays as the adversary brutally sifts! His prayer had been *"that your faith does not fail."* Is this our prayer too, or do we focus on the fault rather than on the faith? Concentrating on our faults can result in undermining us to such a degree that we become worthless in our own eyes, like the ten spies whose perception of God's people was *"we were like grasshoppers in our own sight, and so we were in their sight"* (43). They focused on their weakness, but it wasn't their strength that failed, it was their faith. The lesson to be learned is that the enemy will take advantage by seeing us in the way we see ourselves.

But it's what we are in Christ that matters, and He is *"the author and finisher of faith"* (44). It is through Him that we received faith, for *"faith comes by hearing, and hearing by the word of God"* (45) and it's through Him that *"we walk by faith"* (46). The Lord didn't pray that Peter wouldn't make any more mistakes. No, He prayed for something much deeper: His must-prayer (Gr. *deomai*: to bind oneself or beg – from *deō*, to tie, as in Matthew 21:2; and *dei*: must) centred on the adversary's target, Peter's faith. When we pray for others in difficulty, do we pray as the Saviour prays, synchronising our burden with His?

He penetrated the immediate weakness and saw the real threat, that the Christian's wrestling is not *"against flesh and blood, but ... against spiritual hosts of wickedness in the heavenly places"* (47). In this battle, their mission is not merely to make us make mistakes, it's to cause our mistakes to have such an effect on us that we lose our faith. Our Defence is on the throne, and our victory is in the Victor!

"We rest on Thee, our Shield and our Defender;
We go not forth alone against the foe.
Strong in Thy strength, safe in Thy keeping tender,
We rest on Thee, and in Thy Name we go."
(Edith G. Cherry)

With his faith as the object of his Master's prayer, he was pointed to better days when He said, *"and when you have returned to Me, strengthen your brethren."* Peter had lost sight of his future ministry, but the Lord hadn't. During the three days between Calvary and the resurrection, Peter nursed deep sorrow for he *"wept bitterly"* (48), until the Lord's resurrection brought a change – *"But go, tell His disciples – and Peter"* (49). What grace! This time it was He who introduced the *"But"*, not one of His disciples, and Peter knew that he still had a place in his Saviour's will.

It was no longer Simon, but Peter! The cross had come in between, and the name given at the first was given again to reassure the troubled disciple of a restored relationship. Before the denial, the Lord *"worked effectively"* for Peter in prayer, and after His resurrection He "worked effectively" by comforting him. He worked for *"Peter, an apostle"* – the failing, mistake-ridden apostle – *"of Jesus Christ."* The grace of God had appeared to him once again, just as He does in making *"intercession for"* us (50) *"before the face of God"* (51) that we might serve within the scope of His perfect will by strengthening our brethren.

4. His Discovery

Calvary was Passover time, and Passover time was barley harvest in Israel. The resurrection, fifty days later, was wheat harvest, and Peter became the preacher in the wheat harvest of Pentecost. He was appointed and privileged to witness for his Saviour, and he would have understood if He had set him aside, but *"He who worked effectively in Peter"* kept on proving that the grace of God keeps on appearing and bringing daily salvation to him. At Pentecost, spiritually speaking, he was standing in a very different place.

At Calvary, he stood at the enemy's fire, but at Pentecost he stood up with the eleven with a new fire burning in his heart, actively representing the Lord Jesus Christ. He had promised Peter *"the keys of the kingdom"* (52) and through him a door for the Word (53) was opened in Jerusalem (54), in Samaria (55) and to the Gentiles (56). On that first day in Jerusalem, a wide range of people from different places heard the message (57), and Peter saw thousands coming forward in repentance, being moved by the Holy Spirit who had fallen upon them with *"a sound from heaven, as of a rushing mighty wind"* (58).

They came forward to be baptised as soon as they had been converted. Having *"died with Christ,"* right away they *"were buried with Him through baptism"* (59), and they were added to the first church in Jerusalem – all as the result of the Spirit of God working through Simon Peter's message. What an answer to the Lord having assured him, *"I have prayed for you"*! And now He is doing the same for us. We don't know each other's mistakes, but He does, and He doesn't write us off. He doesn't discard us, because of our defiance; He doesn't dismiss us, because of our unwarranted defence; and He doesn't disown us, because of our unnecessary denial. The One who worked for Peter works for us also.

5. His Disappointment

Going forward in the blessing and power of Pentecost, the word of the Lord came, *"Rise, Peter; kill and eat"* (60). Three commands demanded three responses, but Peter replied, *"Not so, Lord!"* The Holy Spirit took control and, having been reluctant, as it were, to cast the net on the right side of the boat, Peter obeyed and was used by God in taking the gospel to the Gentiles. There had been a threefold rejection, but, yet again, the Lord *"worked effectively"* for Peter.

A woman once approached the late Graham Scroggie at the end of a service to ask his guidance on committing her life to Christ. He turned to Acts 10:14 and pointed out that it's inconsistent to say, as Peter did, *"Not so, Lord"*, since it means objecting to His Lordship. He explained that we can't say all three words in the same sentence and asked her to go home and underline which part she wanted to say. She went back to him later with her Bible open and the word "Lord" underlined, having decided not to say, "Not so".

What about our lives? The Man of Calvary is *"the grace of God"* that has appeared for our sakes, as well as Simon Peter's. We serve on behalf of *"the Apostle and High Priest of our confession ... Jesus"* (61). He is the Apostle who came out from God to speak to man on earth, and He is the High Priest who has gone back in to God to speak for us in heaven. We will discover later how much He meant to Peter in both spheres of His ministry, and in this he is in full agreement with the writer to the Hebrews who loved the name of Jesus so much that he used it nine times.

1. Hebrews 2:9: *"But we see **Jesus**, who was made a little lower than the angels."*
2. Hebrews 3:1: *"Therefore, holy brethren, partakers of the heavenly*

25

calling, consider the Apostle and high Priest of our confession, **Jesus**" (the word Christ is not in the pre-sixth century Greek texts we have).

3. Hebrews 4:14: "*Seeing then that we have a great High Priest who has passed through the heavens, **Jesus** the Son of God.*"

4. Hebrews 6:20: "*where the forerunner has entered for us, even **Jesus**, having become High Priest forever.*"

5. Hebrews 7:22: "*by so much more **Jesus** has become a surety of a better covenant.*"

6. Hebrews 10:19: "*Therefore, brethren, having boldness to enter the Holiest by the blood of **Jesus**.*"

7. Hebrews 12:2: "*Looking unto **Jesus**, the author and finisher of our faith.*"

8. Hebrews 12:24: "*To **Jesus** the Mediator of the new covenant.*"

9. Hebrews 13:12: "*Therefore **Jesus** also, that He might sanctify the people with His own blood, suffered outside the gate.*"

He is the Man of all grace, and Peter would never again say "*Not so*" to Him. After all his ups and downs, he is ready to write his letters to the churches in these five regions of Asia – still answering his Saviour's prayer by strengthening his brethren. Many must have listened to what we read in the first verse and wondered how God ever fitted this man to write such a letter to them. And how is the same God equipping us to take up His inspired Word, including what He has written through Peter, to share the incarnate Word?

Long before Peter's day, God worked through Samson, whom we could think of as the Peter of the Old Testament. Scripture says, "*And the Spirit of the LORD began to move upon him at Mahaneh Dan between Zorah and Eshtaol*" (62). This statement is packed with meaning and shows how God works in the lives of those He calls to shape them into something

26

very different from their old nature. The Spirit *"began"* and the Hebrew word *chalal* tells us something of how He did it for it means to break (63), to wound (64) and includes the thought of putting in a wedge. What a gradual and patient work by the Spirit! He may break and wound Samson, as He used the thin edge of the wedge to begin His gracious work of opening him up to His will, but it was because He wanted *"to move"* him. It means He kept tapping in his life, as if to drive home the wedge that would separate him from his old ways.

Peter knew that the men God used to impart His Word also *"were moved by the Holy Spirit,"* being *carried along* by His power, and we can see how the wedge was beaten into his own experience with the necessary breaking and wounding. His journey was like Samson's who seemed to swing like a pendulum between *"Zorah and Eshtaol."* This is not where Peter lived, yet spiritually he did. Zorah is linked to the thought of being leprous, and Eshtaol means to entreat or to plead. Samson swung between these two extremes, so did Peter, and sometimes so do we. The God of all grace used both men, and we will see how He used Peter as we go farther into his letter.

Undoubtedly, we see much of ourselves in him, but the One who *"worked effectively"* in him wants to work effectively in us too. He *"began"* His good work in us at salvation and will *"complete it until the day of Jesus Christ"* (65). Peter's earthly walk with the Lord began with a look (66) and almost ended with a look (67); it began with a threefold call (68) and ended with a threefold test (69); it began with *"Behold the Lamb of God"* and closed with *"Feed My lambs."* There's no doubt that he discovered what it meant to have 'Grace restored in his mistakes', and so can we!

"Jehovah is our strength, and He shall be our song;
We shall o'ercome at length, although our foes be strong:

In vain doth Satan then oppose, for God is stronger than His foes."
(Samuel Barnard)

(1) 2 Cor.5:20 (2) Matt.2:13-23 (3) Matt.4:18-19 (4) Tit.2:11 (5) Ps.42:7
(6) Jn 21:7, RV, KJV (7) 1 Pet.1:1 (8) Gal.6:1 (9) Jn 13:10 (10) Jn 21:6 (11)
Matt.16:13-16 (12) Lk.7:33 (13) 1 Kin.18:17 (14) Jer.38:4 (15) Matt.9:3 (16)
Ex.3:14 (17) Eph.1:22-23 (18) Matt.16:21-23 (19) Matt.17:4 (20) Matt.5:17;
Lk.24:44 (21) Lk.9:30-31 (22) Lk.9:32 (23) Jn 2:7,11 (24) Lk.9:33 (25)
Lk.9:26 (26) Matt.17:5,8 (27) 1 Pet.5:1 (28) 2 Pet.1:16 (29) Jn 18:6 (30)
Heb.1:3 (31) Matt.26:53 (32) Lk.22:43 (33) Jn 20:12 (34) Matt.16:27 (35)
Lk.22:31-32 (36) Jn 1:42 (37) Jn 18:16 (38) Matt.26:71 (39) Matt.26:73,74
(40) Jn 18:26 (41) 2 Kin.5:26, NASB (42) Jn 2:24-25 (43) Num.13:33 (44)
Heb.12:2 (45) Rom.10:17 (46) 2 Cor.5:7 (47) Eph.6:12 (48) Lk.22:62 (49)
Mk.16:7 (50) Heb.7:25 (51) Heb.9:24, RV (52) Matt.16:19 (53) Col.4:3 (54)
Acts 2 (55) Acts 8:14 (56) Acts 10; 14:27; 15:7 (57) Acts 2:5-11 (58) Acts
2:2,6 (59) Rom.6:1-8 (60) Acts 10:13 (61) Heb.3:1 (62) Judg.13:25 (63)
Ps.89,31,34 (64) Ps.109.22 (65) Phil.1:6 (66) Jn 1:42 (67) Lk.22:61 (68)
Jn 1; Matt.4; Lk.5 (69) Jn 21:15-17

3. GRACE RECEIVED IN THE GOSPEL

Christian living was intensely practical for Peter. It wasn't a theory. There was something about living with the Lord and for the Lord that made him enjoy what Paul called the *"deep things of God"* (1), and he was just as careful to show that they belong *"to the doctrine which accords with godliness"* (2). As far as he was concerned, the teaching must have hands and feet on it, with each aspect being translated into spiritual energy. There was firmness in his conviction, and we get the flavour of this, not only of what he was communicating, but of how he himself enjoyed it. It's good when others get the sense that you're ministering in the enjoyment of what you're talking about, and not just some kind of exercise that leaves them wondering. His letter shows that practical construction depends on spiritual instruction, and that construction must be built on a sound foundation.

This is evident in all five chapters and, although he was addressing believers in these five provinces, God wants us to see that what he was saying also applies to us. They were Jews who had been driven out of their homeland and were now living as foreign residents with new difficulties among Gentiles. In their unsettled state, God gave Peter His own means of comfort by assuring them of how settled they were in Christ. For example, he saw them as:

Elect

His immediate aim was to underline that we are what we are because of the sovereignty of God, just as He was an apostle "of" Jesus Christ, and not only for Him. Their election was according to divine foreknowledge, and he made no attempt to launch into a protracted theological debate. On the contrary: he was way above that, and, as far as he was concerned, he expected them to accept the twofold certainties of their call.

i) It was without question that the call of God began in the heart of God, and in the counsels of Deity in the eternal past. It had then been revealed to them through the cross-work of the Lord Jesus Christ, and their conversion caused them to know that they were chosen in Him.

ii) It was put into effect in time through the work of the Holy Spirit. Paul shared this conviction and was able to say that, *"God from the beginning chose you for salvation through sanctification by the Spirit and belief in the truth, to which He called you by our gospel, for the obtaining of the glory of our Lord Jesus Christ. Therefore, brethren, stand fast"* (3).

It's good to see that these two features are presented as facts by both men through inspiration, and they make it clear that the call is to obedience. Neither these New Testament believers, nor we, were called to salvation alone. No, the work of the Holy Spirit in setting us apart is always with a view to service that is preceded by an initial change. Saving grace wanted only one thing from us, and that was the transfer of our sin to Christ when God laid on Him the iniquity of us all (4). There on the middle cross God fulfilled a work to His own satisfaction that allows believers to live in the full satisfaction of being in Christ. Peter opens his letter by reminding them of where they are geographically and what they are spiritually, then he begins to tell them what they have.

Like them, God has called each of us to:

- A new birth
- A new Owner
- A new nature
- A new intention
- A new direction

Within these, and many other aspects of divine revelation, there *"are some things hard to understand."* For example, the Saviour's incarnation and resurrection, and our regeneration, yet we believe them by faith, even though we still borrow scriptural statements that emphasise our mental limitations.

- Job 42:3: *"I have uttered what I did not understand, things too wonderful for me, which I did not know."*
- Psalm 139:6: *"Such knowledge is too wonderful for me; it is high, I cannot attain it."*
- Psalm 147:5: *"Great is our Lord, and mighty in power; His understanding is infinite."*
- Isaiah 55:8,9: *"For as the heavens are higher than the earth, so are My ways higher than your ways, and My thoughts than your thoughts."*

To put it mildly, we are not able for it, so it's in the limited capacity of our tiny minds that we find room for the huge recognition that God's knowledge is way beyond ours. By Isaiah's measuring scale, the contrast is light years beyond us, so it's only by faith that we trust God and grasp what He has given to us in all we *"have learned and been assured of"* (5). So we thank Him for what we do understand, and trust Him for what we cannot understand. It would be arrogant to claim that our minds can grasp His infinite wisdom. Similarly, it would be arrogance to contest it. Like the smallness of earth in the grand scale of creation, and the temporal before the eternal, we bow at the majesty of God. If, at times, Moses and David could be told they were *lo' tuwkal* – you are not able – we should allow the Holy Spirit to remind us of this as we grapple with truths that are bigger than our minds.

The wonder is, that this sovereign, electing God makes Himself known at all, and Peter tells us how He does it. The very first sentence of his letter speaks of being *"elect"* (6); and it ends by saying, *"Grace to you."* He is so impressed by grace that he closes his letter by calling God *"the God of all grace"* (7). On the same subject, and in the same way, Paul says that God *"chose us in Him"* and adds, *"by grace you have been saved through faith"* (8). This doesn't mean that faith contributes to what God has done. It simply shows that the full hand of God's grace reaches out to the sinner, and the responding empty hand of faith reaches out to receive it.

At the same time, the faith that welcomes His grace should also welcome the accompanying truth of being elect. The grace that chose us means we are fore-chosen; the grace that calls us to be *"before Him in love"* means we are fore-loved; the grace that wills it means we are fore-willed; and the grace that *"made us accepted in the Beloved"* means we are fore-accepted (9).

Isn't it amazing, too, that the faith by which we believe is itself a gift of grace, since it *"comes by hearing, and hearing by the word of God"*? (10). This was expressed by a fifteen-year-old boy in Burma who began his testimony by saying, "God is not a God of partiality. He saved me, a poor Indian boy, not because I wanted to be saved but because He wanted to save me; and He found me, not because I was looking for Him but because He was looking for me."

Foreknowledge

In verse 2, Peter presents God's foreknowledge in relation to the redeemed. In verse 20, he presents the same truth in relation to the Redeemer, but a clear understanding of what it means in regard to Christ will help to prevent us from misunderstanding it in regard to the Christian. Some have claimed that it implies injustice, but how can the One who is both *"just and the justifier of the one who has faith in Jesus"* be unjust? Others reduce its truth to the thought of foresight, but for this to be true with the redeemed we would have to deduce that God chose the Redeemer by looking down the corridor of time to see if He would fulfil His purpose, and in the hope that He would. Thankfully, Scripture helps us to see foreknowledge in the context of how it affected Him.

- Acts 2:23: *"Him, being delivered up by the determined purpose and foreknowledge of God, you have taken by lawless hands, and put to death."*
- Acts 4:27,28: *"For truly against Your holy Servant Jesus, whom You anointed, both Herod and Pontius Pilate, with the Gentiles and the people of Israel, were gathered together to do whatever Your hand and Your purpose determined before to be done."*
- Acts 13:29: *"Now when they had fulfilled all that was written concerning Him, they took Him down from the tree and laid Him in a tomb."*
- Revelation 13:8: *"... the Lamb slain from the foundation of the world."*

These verses confirm this truth in relation to the Saviour who was *"manifest in these last times for you,"* and you will note how perfectly they were fulfilled. Jesus didn't go to Calvary because men took Him there, they took Him because He was going there! Likewise, they pierced His hands and feet because the Scripture said they would. They pierced His side (John 19:37), because Scripture said they would (Zechariah 12:10). But they didn't break His legs, because Scriptures said they wouldn't, and the sovereignty of God is supreme.

The following verses confirm the same great truth of the sovereignty of God in relation to those who are saved:

- Romans 8:29-30: *"For whom He foreknew, He also predestined to be conformed to the image of His Son."*
- Ephesians 1:4,5: *"just as he chose us in Him before the foundation of the world ... having predestined us to adoption as sons by Jesus Christ to Himself."*
- 2 Timothy 1:9: *"God, who has saved us and called us ... according to His own purpose and grace which was given to us in Christ Jesus before time began."*

When we put all these together, we see that God is glorified in how His foreknowledge has been fulfilled in Christ, and He is being glorified again in how His foreknowledge is being fulfilled in each Christian.

Blood

It's not uncommon for believers to describe their security in Christ by saying they are "under the blood", and they say it sincerely. However, God places such a high value on the blood of the Lord Jesus Christ that He never refers to it simply as 'the blood'. Instead, He speaks of the blood of His own, of Christ, of his cross, of Jesus, of the everlasting covenant, of Jesus Christ His Son, of the Lamb; also of His blood, His own blood, and precious blood. Yes, it's a great blessing to be among the Lord's redeemed, and the present joy of our salvation is that we have been brought into a new relationship with the Lord Jesus Christ through

His blood.

In the enjoyment of this, we respond to Peter's vision that God's plan for us is *"for obedience and sprinkling of the blood of Jesus Christ."* Once again, the relationship is through the application of His blood, but this time it isn't the *"shedding of blood"* that we read of in Hebrews 9:22, it's the *"sprinkling of the blood."* It's always God's desire, and Peter's too, that the application of the blood will lead to a sincere appreciation of the blood. This was the case in Moses' day, when shedding the blood of the Passover lamb allowed its application to the doorposts and lintels, but it didn't stop there. God didn't redeem them to leave them where they were. He led them out of their bondage into His freedom, and this made them free to serve Him in a covenant, at an altar, with a book, and a tabernacle. Exodus 24:6-8 paints the picture for us. Moses:

*"took half the blood and put it in basins, and half the blood he **sprinkled on the altar**; then he took the Book of the Covenant and read it in the hearing of the people. And they said, 'All that the LORD has said we will do, and be obedient.' And Moses took the blood, **sprinkled it on the people**, and said, 'This is the blood of the covenant which the LORD has made with you according to all these words.'"*

Hebrews 9:19-21 adds that Moses, *"**sprinkled** both **the book** itself and all the people ... Then likewise he **sprinkled** with blood **the tabernacle** and all **the vessels** of the ministry."* This helps us to see how God combined the altar of God, the people of God, and the Word of God. All this indicates that the people of God (His servants) were united with the altar of God (His service) on the basis of the Word of God (His Scriptures), thus pointing and appointing their direction. Leviticus 1:5 continues the theme by saying, *"He shall kill the bull [the burnt offering] before the LORD, and the priests, Aaron's sons, shall bring the blood and **sprinkle** the blood all around* *on the altar."*

Now we see that the sprinkling of the blood also determined the direction of Aaron's high priestly service. His presence at the altar must be preceded by the presence of the blood. We will notice that the sequence of Peter's teaching is consistent with this Old Testament picture for he links the sprinkling of blood in verse 2 with the blood for redemption in verses 18 and 19 while dealing with our salvation in chapter 1 before developing its subsequent holy and royal priestly service in chapter 2.

The Old Testament theme climaxes in Leviticus 16, which describes Aaron's entrance to the Most Holy place on the Day of Atonement. This meant going through the veil to approach the mercy seat, but in order to do this he must have another veil between him and it, so there had to be a cloud of incense and the sprinkled blood. God's instructions were plain:

*"And he shall put the incense on the fire before the LORD, that the cloud of incense may cover the mercy seat that is on the Testimony, lest he die. He shall take some of the blood of the bull and **sprinkle** it with his finger on the mercy seat on the east side; and before the mercy seat he shall **sprinkle** some of the blood with his finger seven times."*

By sprinkling it before and upon the mercy seat, Aaron intimated the direction he wanted to go. Whether standing outside at the altar or inside at the mercy seat, there must be sprinkled blood at his feet as a God-given platform for his service. In His own unique fulfilment of this, the Lord Jesus Christ answered the sevenfold perfection that was foreshadowed in Aaron's standing when *"with* [Gr. *dia*: through − not with] *His own blood He entered the Most Holy Place once for all, having obtained eternal redemption"* (11).

In these delightful ways, we see that the blood, while essentially the same, is effectively different. Shedding was for cleansing the soul in salvation and deliverance; sprinkling was for the direction of the service and obedience.

Salvation

As we look back on what God had in mind for those He redeemed through the Passover lamb, it's good to know that it's like this for us, too. Christ, our Passover, has been sacrificed for us (12), and God hasn't redeemed us to leave us unmoved from our old place in sin, in the flesh, and in the world. He wants to lead us forward into the freedom of His New Covenant, into the blessings of the cross, His Word, and His service. Peter's approach to the great truth of salvation in the opening chapter is very interesting. In verses 3-12, he speaks of its object – our security in Christ - prospectively. In verses 18-25, he speaks of its origin – our security in Christ - retrospectively.

Each of us can look back to the moment of salvation when we claimed the promise, *"Believe on the Lord Jesus Christ, and you will be saved"* (13). In undeserved grace, our sins were forgiven and we were saved from the penalty of sin. We then began our Christian walk, and the Word of God challenged us to *"work out your own salvation with fear and trembling"* (14). It's evident that Paul isn't referring to the time when we accepted Christ as Lord and Saviour, but to the here and now of our daily witness. He's urging us to reflect what has already happened: we belong to Christ and should have the desire to shine as we show this in the world.

When he talks of becoming *"blameless and harmless,"* he doesn't mean we will be sinless, but that we won't live in such a way that we put up with defects or be content with some sort of admixture. Two things will keep others from pointing the finger: one is that we let God work, so that we do His will and pleasure; the other is that we let the Holy Spirit work, so that He keeps us from doing our own will and pleasure. In other words, this second aspect of our salvation means we need to be saved from the power and pleasure of sin. It's a daily battle, and we don't need to lose it!

Peter then tells us that we are being kept *"for salvation"* (15), and this has to do with the third aspect, that will take place at the coming of the Lord. Then, and only then, will our bodies be delivered from the presence of sin, yet Peter says, it's *"ready to be revealed."* It's to this that Paul refers in Romans 8:23 when speaking about *"the redemption of our body,"* and again in Romans 13:11 when assuring us that *"now our salvation is nearer to us than when we first believed."* If the Lord had come earlier, it was ready. If He were to come today, it's ready. Should His coming not be for a further unknown period, it's ready. The question is, are we? Being at home with the Lord is our promised objective, and anticipating it should spur our Christian character and conduct.

As he points forward to our eternal inheritance, which is the undisputed birthright of every believer, he describes it as "incorruptible", and it's interesting how he uses this word for what God will give us, has given us, and is giving us:

- Incorruptible inheritance (1 Peter 1:4) - **Future**
- Incorruptible seed (1 Peter 1:23) - **Past**
- Incorruptible apparel (1 Peter 3:4) - **Present**

Our inheritance means so much to God that He assures us of it in various ways. It's guaranteed (16), it has glory (17), it's eternal (18) and Peter says it's incorruptible and undefiled (19). Each of these has been deliberately designed to make us thankful for the shedding of the Saviour's blood, and cause us to live in the appreciation of His sprinkled blood. With this in mind, our attention is drawn to the thought that we *"are kept by the power of God through faith for salvation ready to be revealed in the last time"* (20).

The word *"kept"* means guarded in such a way that no external force can take us out of the security we have in Christ. It also means that no internal desire can cause us to leave that security. We are garrisoned, therefore nothing can break in, and no one can break out! This is the ultimate goal and expectation of our salvation. It's the end of the journey when, at last, we will no longer live by faith.

Receiving ... the end of your faith (1 Peter 1:9)

This is the ultimate goal and expectation of our salvation. It's the end of the journey when, at last, we will no longer live by faith. It's one of the great changes that will take place *"in the twinkling of an eye"* (21). In that moment, we will be *"caught up ... to meet the Lord in the air"* (22) we will have new bodies (23) and *"we shall be like Him, for we will see Him as He is"* (24). What a difference! In the reality of His present keeping, and in the sure hope of that future meeting, Peter says, *"you greatly rejoice"* (25). Is that true? It was for those that received his letter, for he went on to say what it would be like for them when their unseeing days were over. He says that, even in the very thought of it, *"you rejoice with joy inexpressible and full of glory."* Do we? Yes, for the up-look is bright, even if the outlook isn't!

It seems strange, at first, that verse 6 should speak about rejoicing and grieving, but they are not incompatible emotions. Was it not so for the Saviour? Did He not grieve in Gethsemane while anticipating the cross and the joy that was set before Him? (26). We rejoice in what lies before us, even though we may grieve over what is beside us. It may be that domestic or secular cares, or some aspect of our spiritual walk, are among the inescapable things that grieve. Nevertheless, God longs to ensure that their presence is for the testing of faith, and not for destroying it.

Grace

Peter loves the word "grace." We will trace it as we go through his letter, and we will see how he applies it in different contexts. As far as chapter 1 is concerned, the riches of God's grace are presented in two ways: sacrificially and eternally.

SACRIFICIAL

He knew that far-seeing prophets had *"prophesied of the grace that would come to you"* (27) and looking back it's evident that there are foreshadowings in the Old Testament of *"the sufferings of Christ and of the glories that would follow"* (28). Thus angels anticipated the demonstration of God's grace in the death of His Son. Not only so, they knew that He would not be bound by death, and prophesied of His resurrection glory. Shortsightedness is not an attribute of the Spirit of God, nor did it belong to men who were led by Him to write as they did. Examples are not in short supply.

- The cross - His sufferings (Psalm 22)
- The crown - His glories (Psalm 24)
- The cross - His sufferings (Isaiah 53:5)
- The crown - His glories (Isaiah 52:13; 53:11)

One of the loveliest figures of this can be found in Numbers 4:13 where we read, *"Also they shall take away the ashes from the altar, and spread a purple cloth over it."* In the very same way as David and Isaiah spoke of the coming One, so also did Moses for the ashes point to the sacrifice completed – the sufferings of Christ; and the purple cloth of His resulting splendour – the glories that would follow.

As we know, Paul wrote to Titus and said, *"For the grace that brings salvation has appeared to all men"* (29) and then he acknowledged the same sacrificial grace by adding, *"looking for the blessed hope and glorious appearing of our great God and Saviour Jesus Christ."* In saying this, he projects our thoughts forward to consider the expression of grace that is:

ETERNAL

Peter's comment on this is *"rest your hope fully upon the grace that is to be brought to you at the revelation of Jesus Christ"* (30). The word *"fully"* (Gr. *teleiōs*: perfectly) means "to the end." At the beginning, we were given *"good hope by grace"* (31) and we face the end resting in the hope of more grace. In verse 10, he spoke of *"the grace"* that was brought to us through the appearing of Christ for the suffering of death. It was in the body that God *"prepared"* for Him that He brought grace *down* to us, and now we look for *"the grace"* that will be brought to us when, in new bodies, we go *up* to meet Him. *"He will appear a second time, apart from sin, for salvation"* (32).

This is what we know as 'The Rapture' when the church will be *"caught up"* (33) at His coming. It is by faith that we *"eagerly wait for Him."* Until then, He continues to give what John describes as *"grace for grace"* (34) – ever-flowing and overflowing, like a river over its bed or waves

41

over a beach. Yesterday's flow is replaced by today's, and today's by tomorrow's, just as today's grace replaces yesterday's in the sure hope of tomorrow's and brings renewed refreshment to the soul. James simply calls it *"more grace"* (35) and Annie Johnson Flint captures this well in her hymn:

"He giveth more grace when the burdens grow greater,
He sendeth more strength when the labors increase;
To added afflictions He addeth His mercy,
To multiplied trials, His multiplied peace.

When we have exhausted our store of endurance,
When our strength has failed ere the day is half done,
When we reach the end of our hoarded resources,
Our Father's full giving is only begun.

Fear not that thy need shall exceed His provision,
Our God ever yearns His resources to share;
Lean hard on the arm everlasting, availing;
The Father both thee and thy load will upbear.

His love has no limits, His grace has no measure,
His power no boundary known unto men;
For out of His infinite riches in Jesus
He giveth, and giveth, and giveth again."

As we trace the riches of God's grace in each chapter, we should never forget that all God's dealings with us began with *"mercy"* (36). The Greek word *eleos* comes from *eleeō*, meaning pity and compassion, and it was in this way that He viewed our miserable sinful condition before granting us the undeserved favour of His grace through which He saved us. It has been said that the difference between mercy and grace is that mercy keeps us from getting what we do deserve, and grace gives us what we don't deserve.

Therefore (1 Peter 1:13)

This is the *"Therefore"* of suitable spiritual activity in response to God's grace. It also is the *"Therefore"* of the unsuitability of carnal activity. It's the *"Therefore"* of commitment to the real terms of godly living, to the personal acceptance of the terms of the New Covenant. Like Aaron, we have communion with the altar in our Saviour's death on the cross; and we have communion with the ark in His resurrection and ascension to the throne.

(1) 1 Cor.2:10 (2) 1 Tim.6:3 (3) 2 Thess.2:13-15 (4) Isa.53:6 (5) 2 Tim.3:14 (6) 1 Pet.1:1,2 (7) 1 Pet.5:10 (8) Eph.1:4;2:8 (9) Eph.1:4-6 (10) Rom.10:17 (11) Heb.9:12 (12) 1 Cor.5:7 (13) Acts 16:31 (14) Phil.2:12-15 (15) 1 Pet.1:5 (16) Eph.1:14 (17) Eph.1:18 (18) Heb.9:15 (19) 1 Pet.1:4 (20) 1 Pet.1:5 (21) 1 Cor.15:52 (22) 1 Thess.4:17 (23) Phil.3:20,21 (24) 1 Jn 3:2 (25) 1 Pet.1:8, NASB (26) Heb.12:2 (27) 1 Pet.1:10 (28) Lk.24:26; 1 Pet.1:11 (29) Tit.2:11,13 (30) 1 Pet.1:13 (31) 2 Thess.2:16 (32) Heb.9:28 (33) 1 Thess.4:16-17 (34) Jn 1:16 (35) Jas.4:6 (36) 1 Pet.1:3

1 Peter 2:25-3:10

"But the word of the Lord endures forever. Now this is the word which by the gospel was preached to you. Therefore, laying aside all malice, all deceit, hypocrisy, envy, and all evil speaking, as newborn babes, desire the pure milk of the word, that you may grow thereby, if indeed you have tasted that the Lord is gracious. Coming to Him as to a living stone, rejected indeed by men, but chosen by God and precious, you also, as living stones, are being built up a spiritual house, a holy priesthood, to offer up spiritual sacrifices acceptable to God through Jesus Christ.

Therefore it is also contained in the Scripture, 'Behold, I lay in Zion a chief cornerstone, elect, precious, and he who believes on Him will by no means be put to shame.' Therefore, to you who believe, He is precious; but to those who are disobedient, 'The stone which the builders rejected has become the chief cornerstone', and 'A stone of stumbling and a rock of offense.' They stumble, being disobedient to the word, to which they also were appointed.

But you are a chosen generation, a royal priesthood, a holy nation, His own special people, that you may proclaim the praises of Him who called you out of darkness into His marvellous light; who once were not a people but are now the people of God, who had not obtained mercy but now have obtained mercy" (1 Peter 1:25–2:10).

4. GRACE REGARDED IN WORSHIP & WITNESS

Up until now, we have been looking at chapter 1, and it's good for us to see how the content of chapter 2 flows out of it. For the most part, we are indebted to those who divided the Scripture into chapters and verses (1), but sometimes we miss the flow by not connecting what we are reading to what has gone before. When we read chapter 2, it's important not to miss its connection with chapter 1. In fact, it's the breakdown that actually helps us to notice something very special for each chapter begins by applying something on earth, and ends by lifting our minds to heaven. We can trace this as follows:

Earthward

- 1:1 *"To the pilgrims of the Dispersion"*
- 2:1 *"Laying aside all malice"*
- 3:1 *"Wives"*
- 4:1 *"Christ suffered for us"*
- 5:1 *"The elders"*

Heavenward

- 1:25 *"The word of the Lord endures forever"*

- 2:25 *"The Shepherd and Overseer of your souls"*
- 3:22 *"Jesus Christ, who has gone into heaven"*
- 4:19 *"Commit your souls ... as to a faithful Creator"*
- 5:11 *"To Him be the glory"*

If only our lives were lived in this wonderful combination of something heavenly being seen in each aspect of our earthly walk!

The Word of the LORD

As Peter moves on from his introduction, we can follow a progression that reflects what happened under Moses the mediator of the Old Covenant. One parallel is seen in chapter 1:19 in the fulfilment of the Passover lamb of Exodus 12, and in chapter 2's fulfilment of the anticipation of priestly service in Exodus 24. We also can see the death of Lord Jesus Christ being the answer to the tabernacle's altar, just as the Word answers to what was foreshadowed in the laver. The altar was the first thing that offerers met when they came in through the gateway. There was heat and light, and beyond that there was the laver constantly reflecting the flame of the altar that was mirrored outside in its copper and in the water inside. It was just as if it was on fire too.

Being side by side, they remind us of the close relationship there is between the incarnate Word and the inspired Word. And isn't it wonderful how God again exalted His Word when *"Moses commanded the Levites that bore the ark of the covenant of the LORD, saying: Take this Book of the Law, and put it beside the ark of the covenant of the LORD your God"* (2). These dear men shouldered the ark and the Law, and they teach us that those who would bear a testimony to the Lord Jesus Christ must also be carriers of His Word.

Peter has been absorbed by God's grace in chapter 1, which was brought to us firstly through the death of the Lord Jesus Christ, and will be brought again when He is revealed at His coming (3). Having drawn out our appreciation of sacrificial and eternal grace, Peter then draws out our appreciation of the Word through which we were born again (4), and he gives it a lofty place. As the Word of God, it bears the hallmark of His Deity; as the Word of the LORD, it declares His authority; and by living and abiding forever, it presents His eternity.

In these three characteristics it amply represents the God who gave it. This isn't surprising for, in one sense, the Word of God is more connected to heaven than it is to earth. It's for earth, but was breathed out from heaven, so we can understand why Peter wants us to know that everything we are and have is Word-based. It deserves our deepest appreciation and lifelong appropriation. God has magnified His Word above all His name (5), it is forever settled in heaven (6), and ought to be magnified and settled in our lives too.

Quite rightly, we make a lot of chapter two, but we would automatically make more of it if we made more of chapter one. Perhaps, we miss out by not sufficiently recognising that what we are doing for the Lord Jesus in chapter 2 is the direct result of all that we have in Him in chapter 1. It tells us about the promise of the presence of the Lord with us on earth, and includes the additional promise of our presence with Him in heaven. In a very remarkable way, what we see at the beginning and end of each chapter aptly describes what Peter does in the themes and doctrines throughout his letter. They unite heaven and earth, and that's not accidental. He wants to us see that appreciation of salvation in chapter 1 leads on to the appreciation of service in chapter 2.

Paul does the same in Ephesians and, once again, we may give more emphasis to the end of chapter 2 where we read about *"a dwelling place of God in the Spirit."* Paul uses the Greek word *katoikētērion*, which can be translated as a down-dwelling or a down-residence, and its beauty is that this down-habitation should resemble and reflect *"the church, which is His body, the fulness of Him who fills all in all"* (7). It's a high standard, but the church is the heavenly template for churches on earth.

Desire the Pure Milk of the Word

As Christians, we should have a yearning, a real soul longing, for the Word. Just as it's natural for newborn infants instinctively to crave feeding, the newborn child of God should instinctively desire being fed from the Scriptures. Peter's first reason for saying this is that our growth depends on it; so we really need to ask ourselves if we are growing. God has given the means, yet some believers suffer from a kind of spiritual malnutrition because they never develop a hunger for His Word.

Feeding is a lifestyle, and being spiritually healthy demands regularly taking time to read our Bibles. Just as it is naturally, feeding is a necessity, and we should be crying out, *"Feed me with the food that is needful for me"* (8). The real force of what Peter's advice is, is to keep on desiring the Word. It won't happen by being haphazard. If we take good care of it, the Spirit of God will take care of our growth; and, if we allow Him to take care of our growth, we will discover that reading feeds our worship.

It's all part of the kind of progress that Paul wanted to see in young Timothy, and to help him on his way Paul gave him the recipe. His first ingredient was, *"Give attention to reading"* (9). This is normally taken as public reading, but Timothy's public reading must have been the result of what he enjoyed in his private reading. There's a massive lesson in this: none of us will ever be more publicly than we are privately. This is so vital, we should say it again: none of us will ever be more publicly than we are privately. Don't ever for a minute tell yourself that you can get away with bluffing your audience. God is sovereign, and His Spirit's power accompanies those who pay attention to being real in private.

Time spent reading is at its most profitable when we *"meditate on these things."* This was Paul's fifth ingredient, after emphasising that reading enables exhortation, the understanding of doctrine, and the development of gift. Meditation has different connotations, of course. Gurus of many complexions say it means emptying your mind, but this is entirely the opposite of what God means by it. To Him, it means filling the mind. One of the words He uses in the Old Testament – in Hebrew, *siyach* – means to muse or ponder, and actually describes a shrub in Genesis 21:15. The idea is of the initial stem branching out as it grows, and this is a lovely way of seeing how an initial thought leads off into many branches of wider consideration. It can be a long process, but not arduous.

The enjoyment is captured in the other word God uses – *hagah* – which describes a lion roaring over its prey (10). When we enjoy it like this, we will be able to tell God, *"I rejoice at Your word as one who finds great treasure"* (11) and He wants to be the first to hear of it from you.

Worship

As far as Peter is concerned, our appreciation and application of grace will bring us into what he goes on to outline regarding worship and witness, and immediately he connects our service on earth with our access to heaven. Worshippers are described as *"living stones,"* born-again believers who have already come once as individuals to Christ for salvation, and in this character we are *"being built up a spiritual house, a holy priesthood, to offer up spiritual sacrifices acceptable to God through Jesus Christ."* Once again, we are *"coming to Him,"* but this time we are coming collectively and, since the word *proserchomenoi* is plural and in the present tense, it means we are constantly coming to Him in worship.

Joy of all joys, we are coming to Him in Zion, that is into heaven. When the sons of Korah thought about coming before God, they spoke of hearts being set on the pilgrimage, and of each one appearing before God in Zion (12). Jeremiah pointed to a future day when, in the presence of Christ their Messiah, *"They shall come and sing in the height of Zion, streaming to the goodness of the LORD"* (13). The word *"streaming"* means to flow or to sparkle, like a river shining in the sun to such a degree that the sight of the water is lost and replaced by a reflection of sheer glory. It means to be so cheerful that you glow. The thought of a flowing, glowing river is exactly what God wants to see as we gather for worship.

If the people of Israel could have such pleasure in coming to Zion on earth, how much more should we as we flow to Zion above? When we flow into His presence, heaven sees the reflection of the One with whom we have lived for the previous seven days. Radiating from our hearts is the gleam of exaltation from those who are boasting in their risen Saviour. Defying the gravity of earthly things, we flow upward as worshippers with our praises merging, and heaven rejoicing in the bright reflection of the Son. Wouldn't that be marvellous? Thrill of all thrills!

But how do we go about it? It means that we have to be prepared beforehand. David tells us how to come: *"Give to the Lord the glory due to His name; bring an offering, and come before Him. Oh, worship the LORD in the beauty of holiness"* (14). His order was *"Give ... bring ... come"*; but we reverse the order as we prepare to worship, and we come, bring, and give. This is how we should be ready to enter God's presence, but we will catch the sense of giving Him glory only if we have come and are truly ready to glory in Christ Jesus.

The writer to the Hebrews puts it this way: *"having boldness to enter the Holiest by the blood of Jesus ... let us draw near"* and *"by Him let us continually offer the sacrifice of praise to God"* (15). This is called *"the fruit of our lips,"* but why does God use such an analogy? It means He is looking for the ultimate purpose of the tree. All its energy and growth has been poured into producing fruit, and this represents the fruitfulness that should be evident in our thoughts and words as we worship Him. We don't bring twigs, and we don't bring leaves. God is waiting for the fruit of our meditation, and we should approach Him saying, *"Let the words of my mouth and the meditation of my heart be acceptable in Your sight, O LORD, my strength and my Redeemer"* (16).

A fellow-believer came to me one Lord's Day and asked, "Tell me what was different between what you were doing this morning and what I was doing this morning?" I said, "My brother, the last thing I'm here to do is to demean what you did this morning. It's not my business to downplay what you did this morning, but let me ask you one thing. Where did you go?" He said, I went to the Hall." "And what did you do when you went to the Hall?" "Well, we worshipped." He then asked me, "So what did you do?" I replied, "I went to heaven." In surprise, he said, "Come on! What do you mean?" I said, "Let's have a look at Hebrews 9 verse 12 – *"that the Lord Jesus through his own blood entered into the Most Holy Place once for all, having obtained eternal redemption."* I said, "Brother, where would that be?" "Oh", he says, "that's heaven."

"Well, let's look over the page at chapter 10 verse 19 – *"Therefore, brethren, having boldness to enter into the Holiest by the blood of Jesus."* I stopped reading and asked him, "Where would that be?" Right away, he said, "Well, I never saw that before."

Peter is showing us the very same thing and, in doing so, takes us back to the cause of it all: we have tasted that the Lord is gracious. Now, we could assume that this is another precious aspect of God's grace in Peter's letter, but it's not. Instead of the word *charis* he has used the word *chrēstos*, which refers to the Lord's goodness, just as Paul did in Romans 2:4 when he asked, *"Do you despise the riches of His goodness ... not knowing that the goodness of God leads you to repentance?"* In the selfsame kindness that led us as sinners to repentance, God leads us into His presence as worshippers, to worship by the Spirit of God and glory in Christ Jesus (17).

Later, in chapter 4:10, Peter uses the phrase *charitos Theou* to speak about the grace of God, but here he actually says *"chrēstos ho kurios"*, which means "the Lord is gracious" or "the Lord is good." He doesn't want us to miss the connection that verse 3 provides, as it reaches back into chapter 1 and forward to our worship in chapter 2. Our union with the "good Lord" is the basis of our communion, and fellowship is the basis of our worship.

What is Worship?

- It's presenting the worth of Christ to God. The Old English spelling was *worthship*, and this means we are engaged in thinking about what God thinks about Him. True *worthship* is thinking lofty thoughts of Christ.
- It's the whole being, all that we are, rejoicing in the worth of the Lord Jesus Christ. It's every part of us – body, soul and spirit –

united in enthusiastic praise of the Saviour.

- It's a holy excitement in the presence of God, when our spirits are raised and we cannot rest until the mouth expresses what the heart feels. So it's definitely not flattery (18).
- It's an attitude of homage and adoration. The word includes the thought of crouching down in His presence like a dog licking the hand of its master.
- It's having the tongue of a ready writer with thoughts flowing from the heart. But they will never flow out if they never flowed in, and they will never flow in unless we have daily communion with the Lord. How vital it is that we learn to ask, "Where do You want us to prepare?"

If only we could gather in that kind of spirit, we would not only move one another, we would move Him! Do you ever wonder if heaven has been moved by our worship? When we read Revelation chapter 5 there's a pulsating sense of worship in the presence of God as the four living creatures, the elders and the angelic host are affected in their posture by the song that has been sung. All heaven is thrilled: touched by worshippers from earth.

Do we ever wonder what they feel when it comes to the time of our drawing near and they watch the Man in the midst receiving what we place in His hands? Since they can be so moved, can they sense our mediocrity too? Do they ever say to one another, "Is that the best they can do? He never went to the cross for me, yet that's all they gave! He never died for me, yet I give more than that!" What a sad possibility that heaven isn't moved by present worship from the redeemed of earth!

What is Worship Not?

In chapter 22 of the first book of our Bible, when Abraham took Isaac to Moriah, he told his servants, *"The lad and I will go yonder and worship."* In chapter 22 of the last Book, the angel told John, *"Worship God."* The Scriptures have much to teach us about worship, and one of the things we learn is that the word "worship" is sometimes a verb, sometimes a noun, but never an adjective. This has been turned around in much of what is called worship in the present day. It's not unusual to hear of, 'Worship Leaders ... Worship Leader Training Manual ... Worship Leader Online Academy ... and Worship Team Building', with each of them using worship as an adjective. We are not condemning the appropriate God-honouring use of music, but perhaps we should bow to the definition given by its Designer.

Witness

Alongside our access to God as a worshipping holy priesthood, we also have access to people as a witnessing royal priesthood. What a privilege it is, that we are called to live in the character of the holiness and majesty of God! It's not that we cease to be a holy priesthood when our times of collective worship are over, or that we are no longer a royal priesthood when we are not sharing the gospel. The truth is, we are worshipping as we witness and witnessing while we worship. Paul makes this clear in two ways.

Firstly, our lives are spent in spiritual worship when we present our bodies as a living sacrifice (19). He also tells us that, *"We are to God the fragrance of Christ among those who are being saved and among those who are perishing"* (20). The illustration behind Paul's words is very meaningful. It depicts a returning army, probably with its generals at the head. In front of them were the incense swingers leading a parade of victorious soldiers, behind whom were enemy prisoners that had been taken captive. As the incense wafted its savour, it had two different effects. To the victors, it was of *"life to life"*; to the losers, it was of *"death to death."*

Whenever we read of fragrance in the Scriptures, it often has to do with the aroma that ascends to God from sacrifice, and we can see this again in 2 Corinthians 2:15–17. When Paul says *"we are a fragrance to God of Christ,"* that's worship. When he says, *"we speak in the sight of God"*, that's witness, and it's significant that the worship part is "to God" and the witness part is "from God." Together, they show that worship and witness go hand in hand.

Secondly, as we remember Him and worship together, we *"proclaim the Lord's death till He comes"* (21). It's a testimony to others, and a very meaningful witness as we worship. Although it's a proclamation to fellow-worshippers, it also is to any who hear and see what is being said and done. This widens into a proclamation of Christ's excellencies and virtues, as we share the glories of Him who calls His own *"out of darkness into His marvellous light."*

Let our prayer be that God will see Christ in what we say, and then when we go outside that others might see Christ in what we say. This is the ministry of worship that's upwards and Godward and heavenward, and it's also the ministry of witness that's outward and manward and earthward. May it be so, for His Name's sake.

(1) The divisions in most versions of the Bible were introduced by Stephen Langton, Archbishop of Canterbury (1207-28), and Robert Estienne added verses in 1551. (2) Deut.31:26 (3) 1 Pet.1:10,13 (4) 1

Pet.1:23 (5) Ps.138:2 (6) Ps.119:89 (7) Eph.1:22,23 (8) Prov.30:8, ESV (9) 1 Tim.4:13-16 (10) Isa.31:4 (11) Ps.119:162 (12) Ps.84:5,7 (13) Jer.31:12 (14) 1 Chron.16:29 (15) Heb.10:19-22; Heb.13:15 (16) Ps.19:14 (17) Phil.3:3 (18) Ps.5:9; Ps.78:36; Mk.7:6 (19) Rom.12:1 (20) 2 Cor.2:15 (21) 1 Cor.11:26

1 Peter 2:11-25

"Beloved, I beg you as sojourners and pilgrims, abstain from fleshly lusts which war against the soul, having your conduct honourable among the Gentiles, that when they speak against you as evildoers, they may, by your good works which they observe, glorify God in the day of visitation. Therefore submit yourselves to every ordinance of man for the Lord's sake, whether to the king as supreme, or to governors, as to those who are sent by him for the punishment of evildoers and for the praise of those who do good. For this is the will of God, that by doing good you may put to silence the ignorance of foolish men— as free, yet not using liberty as a cloak for vice, but as bondservants of God.

Honour all people. Love the brotherhood. Fear God. Honour the king. Servants, be submissive to your masters with all fear, not only to the good and gentle, but also to the harsh. For this is commendable, if because of conscience toward God one endures grief, suffering wrongfully. For what credit is it if, when you are beaten for your faults, you take it patiently? But when you do good and suffer, if you take it patiently, this is commendable before God.

For to this you were called, because Christ also suffered for us, leaving us an example, that you should follow His steps: "Who committed no sin, nor was deceit found in His mouth"; who, when He was reviled, did not revile in return; when He suffered, He did not threaten, but committed Himself to Him who judges righteously; who Himself bore our sins in His own body on the tree, that we, having died to sins, might live for righteousness— by whose stripes you were healed. For you were like sheep going astray, but have now returned to the Shepherd and Overseer of your souls" (1 Peter 2:11-25).

5. GRACE REINFORCED IN TRIALS

It's never a random work when God scatters. Men may scatter destructively to achieve their purpose, but God does it constructively to achieve
His. There's evidence of both kinds of scattering during the days of
the Acts. When Gamaliel spoke about the death of Theudas in Acts
5:36, he states that his followers were scattered and came to nothing.
They came to nothing, and their scattering – *dieluthēsan* – means the
whole movement dissolved. Another revolt, led by Judas of Galilee, also
came to a fruitless end when he was killed and they were scattered –
dieskorpisthēsan – like sheep scattered in disarray by a wolf. It's no
accident that this is the word applied to the disciples when the Lord said,
"you will be scattered, each to his own, and will leave Me alone" (1). On that
occasion, their scattering was of the flesh and not a work of God.

In Acts 8:1, it was very different, for this scattering was His means
of spreading His children into regions away from Jerusalem, and He
consistently refers to this scattering as *diaspeiro*. It was as if he blew
them like seed that was being sown farther afield, and this is exactly the
kind of scattering that James and Peter speak about at the beginning
of their letters (2). In all these, God was working to fulfil the Lord's
promise in Acts 1:8, *"you shall be My witnesses in Jerusalem, and in all
Judea and Samaria, and to the ends of the earth."*

During the time when work of rebuilding the temple ceased in the days of Ezra, a promise was given through Zechariah the prophet. There had been singing and shouting when the foundation stones were laid, but he encouraged the people by assuring them that the headstone would finish the work, and that it would be brought out with shouts of *"Grace, grace to it!"* (3). Perfect grace, multiplied grace, shown in days of law. What triumph! Haggai and Zechariah were great men of God, and they encouraged the people. Haggai did it by urging the people to work. Zechariah never mentioned the word "work". His ministry was different; he did it by pointing the people to the Man.

In chapter 1:10 and 11, He is the Man who stood among the myrtle trees, as the Angel of the LORD, and this is known as a Theophany or a Christophany, a pre-incarnate appearing of the Lord Jesus Christ (4). In Zechariah 6:12, God urged His people to look at Him as *"the Man whose name is the BRANCH!"* In chapter 13:7, He points them to the cross through the words of God the Father speaking about God the Son, *"Awake, O sword, against My Shepherd, against the Man who is My Companion ... Strike the Shepherd and the sheep will be scattered."* Ever since Calvary, the Jew has been scattered, but a day of gathering will come and, in preparing them for millennial glory in the presence of their Messiah, they will look unto Him whom they have pierced (5). Their days of scattering will be over.

To Peter, his readers were scattered pilgrims, and he said this literally of them because they were foreign residents in a place that wasn't home. But, even then, he was assuring them that God in His grace had uprooted and scattered them into areas where the gospel would take root and develop. This is the point he develops in chapter 2:11, but this time he calls them sojourners and pilgrims and applies it spiritually. As Christians, they are foreigners in a world that is alien to them, and they to it. As strangers, geographically, in some ways they would have to adapt, but now he is telling them that they are strangers, spiritually, and that they had not to adapt.

To encourage them, he pointed, not to something on earth in Jerusalem, but to Someone in heaven. He lifted their eyes of faith to see the risen Lord Jesus Christ, the *"living stone,"* that they might see Him as the One whom God has laid *"in Zion as the chief cornerstone."* And they could cry, *"Grace, grace"* to Him with the assurance that grace would cause them to triumph in their trials.

It's worth noting that chapter 1 begins and ends with birth, and chapter 2 begins with growth. We could say that chapter 1 is about the deliverance of the sinner, and chapter 2 is about the direction of the believer. Chapter 1 is about coming to Christ for salvation, forgiveness, and conversion; chapter 2 is about coming to Him in service, fellowship, and commitment. There are other considerations too: in chapter 1, we have the sacrifice, sufferings and submission of Christ; in chapter 2, we read of the sacrifices, the sufferings and submission of the believer. All of these need grace. In chapter 2, we discover our need of grace as worshippers and as witnesses and we need to produce the evidence of it in our walk. We need it in spiritual service toward God in the Holy Place, and we need it as servants of men in the workplace.

However, the real lesson for us to learn is that if God supplies grace sacrificially and eternally, then we should let Him apply it experientially and daily. We could even make a case for using the word 'experimentally' for it conveys the thought of something tested, as in a science lab, that proves the theory and leads us to end up with the intended conclusion. Either way, God wants us to experience His grace and He does it by proving, not only the availability, but the applicability to help us in every aspect of growth.

It would be a very strange person who was satisfied with a child that never grew. Would we not feel the same with a child of God? Do we not think there's something seriously wrong when we see a child of God who doesn't grow? God has done everything to make our growth a reality, yet sometimes we don't allow Him to make it a possibility. Let's think of three ways in which His grace enables our spiritual growth.

Through Discipleship

When we come to think of how God helps us to grow in grace, we discover that He often uses the avenue of discipleship. The Lord's parting words at the end of Matthew 28 reinforce this: *"Go therefore and make disciples of all the nations, baptizing them in* [into, RV] *the name of the Father and of the Son and of the Holy Spirit, teaching them to observe all things that I have commanded you."* By saying this, He left us in no doubt that disciples teaching disciples is an effective means of growth. But what makes a good teacher? The Lord Jesus Christ obviously meant that disciples should understand what He had commanded and be able to pass this on to others. So there's a need for teaching disciples to understand His Word, and a complementary need for learning disciples not to expect Word-less growth.

Through Fellowship

The early churches were well schooled. Paul says, *"I kept nothing back that was helpful, but proclaimed it to you, and taught you publicly and from house to house"* (6). When two of his friends, Aquila and Priscilla, heard Apollos teach, they took him privately and *"explained to him the way of God more accurately"* (7). This is a valuable service that disciples can do

63

for each other, and it takes grace to help someone who already speaks accurately to speak more accurately. There is never a shortage of public and private opportunity, and it's in the provision of God's grace that our times of fellowship together as churches are intended to fulfil a teaching ministry.

This is the real impact of Acts 2:42 where those who were saved, baptised and added to the church in Jerusalem continued steadfastly in the apostles' teaching and fellowship, in the breaking of bread, and in the prayers. These four are inseparably blended for our good and for our growth, and it's helpful to see that God intends that we adhere to them all. It also means we have fellowship with all: we have fellowship in teaching, fellowship when we meet to break bread, and also when the assembly gathers for prayer. All of them combine as a unified means of teaching and of learning.

Another aspect of fellowship is presented in Galatians 6:6 – *"Let him who is taught the word share in all good things with him who teaches."* This takes us into the wider expressions of grace that accompany actual teaching, and helps us to recognise that there's more to teaching than explaining something. Sharing in all good things really means having fellowship through teaching by example; by acts of kindness, thoughtfulness, and generosity. These are the additional evidences of grace, which prove that teaching doesn't stand alone.

Through Headship

The headship of Christ is of great value to God, and is to us too. It also is humbling for us and honouring for Him, since His headship presents His preeminence in five ways:

- In His relationship to God (1 Corinthians 11:3)
- In His relationship to all principality and power (Colossians 2:10)
- In His relationship to the church, which is His body (Ephesians 5:23)
- In His relationship over all things to the church (Ephesians 1:22)
- In His relationship to the spiritual house in service (1 Peter 2:7)

In the Old Testament, the word for "head" is *ro'sh* and can be linked to the conspicuous head of a poppy, and there's no doubt that His place within the Trinity is demonstrated in His supremacy over all creation and created beings, His church and over the house. His headship ought to be conspicuous as it's presently being made known:

- Through every saved man and woman's submission, witnessed on earth and by angels (8)
- Through the manifold wisdom of God being made known to the principalities and powers by the church (9)
- As each local assembly fulfils its resemblance to the church, which is His body, and through living stones serving together in union and communion with the Head of the corner (10)

Some versions translate verse 7 as *"chief cornerstone,"* but *kefalēn gōnias* is more accurately translated as "head of the corner," and we should be humbled to think that God has willed the supremacy and authority of Christ to be shown through us.

One way of showing this is in our spiritual growth for we are called to *"grow up in all things into Him who is the Head – Christ"* (11). What a glorious invitation! Brothers and sisters, we have the opportunity of growing up into Him, but this happens only as we draw nourishment down from Him. How blessed we are, that we can be fed by Him, *"from whom all the body, nourished and knit together by joints and ligaments, grows with the increase from God"* (12). We are in touch with the Head, and we reflect this eternal union as we enjoy Him as the head of the corner. As individuals, and as churches, we can thrive in Him and for Him.

Our Example

As we think about assemblies resembling His church, Peter grips our attention as he implies that we can grow in our likeness to Christ by seeing Him as our "example." Resemblance has two sides to it, of course: we can grow in the likeness of Him by absorbing character that we see in Him, but this goes hand in hand with abandoning features we have that are not in Him. He loves righteousness and hates iniquity (13), and we need to be like that too. Some of the old Puritans used to say, "We have learned to equivocate ... Our convictions sit easily about us like an old lady's loose gown. Righteousness has lost its wholesome sternness. The other side of love is hate, but we do not love truth so ardently that we hate a lie. We are too casual. We need His sense of right and wrong, of black and white."

As our perfect example, the Lord Jesus never had anything to hide. One thing is certain: as worshippers, nothing is hidden from God. However, as witnesses, we can hide things from others. Having spoken about worship and witness, Peter suddenly changed course to speak about *"fleshly lusts which war against the soul."* Oh, this is where it can be hard to grow in grace, isn't it? So how do we let it grow? It's partly by deciding not to grow in the things that satisfy the wrong kind of appetite.

Our desire for grace causes us to shun everything else, so he uses the word "abstain." He doesn't say that we should cut it down; he says we should cut it out. The last thing we should want is a walk that weakens our worship and witness. We don't have the desire of the unsaved for we belong to Christ and have crucified the flesh with its passions and desires (14), so how we walk, and with whom we walk, and where we walk are all indications of how we treat the grace of God.

This is Commendable

In the modern world, everyone has rights. There are human rights, civil rights, social rights, workers' rights, childrens' rights, and the right to protest. Being assertive is seen as commendable, but this is a long way from 1 Peter 2's view that being submissive is commendable. In the face of justice or injustice from governments or employers, the Christian has further opportunity to grow in grace. Peter loves the word *charis* so much he used it ten times in his letter, and we find it in each of the five chapters.

However, it's more difficult to find in chapter 2 for the simple reason that none of the main versions translates the word *charis* as grace in verse 19. There's a list of variations – acceptable, approved, a credit to you, commendable, favour, gracious, thankworthy – yet Peter simply says, *"For this is grace, if because of conscience toward God one endures grief, suffering wrongfully."* In a very different way from the world, we may suffer for our rights, but we need to know what they are. There are four defining characteristics of our rights:

- In verse 13, for the Lord's sake
- In verse 15, for the will of God
- In verse 19, for this is grace
- In verse 19, for conscience toward God

If we feel that we suffer for conscience' sake, we have three litmus tests:

- Is my response for the Lord's sake?
- Is it according to the will of God?
- Does it demonstrate the grace of God?

If the answer to all three is, 'Yes', then we have a right – to submit. Submission is our only God-given right, but never protest. There will be times when reasoned discussion is possible, but we must never give way to aggression.

There may be times when the world's 'freedom of speech' approach lures believers into offending God in their attitude to government. There's no doubt that some laws go against the Word of God and violate consciences, but this is not new. The psalmist's comment in Psalm 94:20 must have been relevant in his day, yet we can ask with him, "Shall the throne of iniquity, which devises evil by law, have fellowship with you?" The thought of fellowship has no appeal, but neither does the thought of fighting battles.

When lawmakers present perverse things, where sinful things are put on the statute book, as citizens of these countries we have decisions to make. How do we handle it? Do we protest? Do we get up in arms? God says we should pray and submit. It was far from easy for Christians in the days of the early churches. Brutality was commonplace, as was immorality, yet God's word through Paul was: *"Let every soul be subject to the governing authorities. For there is no authority except from God, and the authorities that exist are appointed by God. Therefore whoever resists the authority resists the ordinance of God, and those who resist will bring judgment on themselves"* (15).

> "God everywhere hath sway,
> And all things serve His might;

His every act pure blessing is,

His path unsullied light."

(Paul Gerhardt)

Chapter 2 of Peter's letter brings us into definite areas of trial for which God has provided the means of grace and, irrespective of what it may be, the Spirit of God is able to give comfort. It may be, as you read this, there is a burden that burns into your very being and you may not have the slightest understanding of why our great God would permit it in the first place. As you bring yourself before His sovereignty and to the safety of His Word, in that Spirit you join with others in whom the grace of God is being reinforced. Whatever your trial is, in grief or in loss, in bereavement, unemployment, or some inward struggle against sin, bring it to the Saviour and, in the sanctifying effect of His Word say, "God, in the name of the Lord Jesus Christ, by Your Spirit, please reinforce Your grace."

Even as Peter's ink was drying on the page, the Spirit of God was directing believers to the Example. In many ways, He suffered wrongfully. He lived, and died, with injustice, yet never committed sin, nor was deceit found in His mouth. This was how He reacted to all sorts of abuse: no wrong thoughts, and no wrong threats. Instead, He surrendered to God who judges righteously. After all that, *"He bore our sins in His own body on the tree, that we, having died to sins, might live for righteousness"* (16) – and not resort to sinful reactions. By seeing Him as our example, we follow His steps. And this will be *charis para Theō(i)* – grace with God.

(1) Jn 16:32 (2) Jas.1:1; 1 Pet.1:1 (3) Zech.4:7 (4) See Gen.18:1,2; Ex.3:2; Judg.6:11-24 (5) Zech.12:10, RVM (6) Acts 20:20 (7) Acts 18:25,26 (8) 1 Cor.11:10 (9) Eph.3:10 (10) 1 Cor.12:27; 1 Pet.2:6,7 (11) Eph.4:15 (12) Col.2:19 (13) Heb.1:9 (14) Gal.5:24 (15) Rom.13:1,2 (16) 1 Pet.2:24

1 Peter 3:1-7

"Wives, likewise, be submissive to your own husbands, that even if some do not obey the word, they, without a word, may be won by the conduct of their wives, when they observe your chaste conduct accompanied by fear. Do not let your adornment be merely outward — arranging the hair, wearing gold, or putting on fine apparel — rather let it be the hidden person of the heart, with the incorruptible beauty of a gentle and quiet spirit, which is very precious in the sight of God. For in this manner, in former times, the holy women who trusted in God also adorned themselves, being submissive to their own husbands, as Sarah obeyed Abraham, calling him lord, whose daughters you are if you do good and are not afraid with any terror. Husbands, likewise, dwell with them with understanding, giving honour to the wife, as to the weaker vessel, and as being heirs together of the grace of life, that your prayers may not be hindered" (1 Peter 3:1-7).

6. GRACE RECIPROCATED IN MARRIAGE

With a stroke of Peter's pen, God turns inward to have a right good look at our home-life and consider how grace can be demonstrated there. Under the care and guidance of His grace, God leads us **upward** in our worship, **outward** in our walk before the world and in our work, and now he moves **inward** to our homes.

At this stage, we can see what God has done for us in chapter 1 of Peter's letter has opened the door into chapter 2, and now we are about to discover that what we read in chapter 2 opens the door into chapter 3. This makes us look back on our salvation with a real sense of thankfulness that chapter 1 is ours. We live and rejoice in the grandeur of His salvation from its beginning in His eternal purpose to its end in His eternal presence. Well could we write over it, *"From everlasting to everlasting, You are God"* (1) for it begins in eternity past with a God who elects, and points us to eternity future to anticipate our predestination.

Next, Peter leads us into chapter 2 where we learn about grace that causes us to handle the delights of worship and witness, alongside the difficulties of suffering wrongfully for doing what's right. By this avenue of worship and witness, our walk in the world and at work, Peter suddenly says, *"Wives."* This means that the God who brought us into His house in chapter 2, and up to the Shepherd and Overseer of our souls, now comes down to our house in chapter 3 and, just as He welcomes us into His house, He wants us to welcome Him into ours. The One who brings us into the precinct of His dwelling place in heaven waits for us to bring Him into the precinct of our homes on earth. By doing this, we permit the One who is at home in our hearts to be the One who also is at the heart of our homes.

He has such a practical way of helping us see that our lives are not broken into compartments with differing behaviour going on in each. Far from it! They are components interlinked by the consistent theme of grace, and we are left in no doubt at all that as children of God and churches, our commitment and conduct, plus our conscientiousness at work are all dependent on us *"desiring the pure milk of the word."* It will take the enjoyment of reading the Scriptures at home to safeguard us from showing a different face at church from what others see at work. Otherwise, it will be very easy to live one way at church and then be a different kind of person elsewhere.

Home is the place where we either decide to put things right or where we drop our guard and let things slip. Preparing our homes for Him means more than preparing its rooms as we might do for a guest, it means the preparation of ourselves. This means seeing how we live, and actively engaging in our communion with Him in our homes. It's the interaction of father, mother, and children being a family who live in such a way that He is able to see things that are consistent with what we are at church. At the end of a church service, a Christian woman was approached by another who wanted to compliment her, because her husband was such a good preacher. Even as she listened to the praise that was being heaped on him, she couldn't help thinking about his abusive ways and saying to herself, "If only you knew what he's like at home."

Some of us may be single. Irrespective of that, God still wants to look in our homes. He wants to look inside the marriage home – He wants to be able to see to what extent we have grown in the grace and knowledge of our Lord. Jesus Christ as individuals, as couples, and as families. This brings us to think of grace in a way that is …

MARITAL

The introduction of grace to our lives in salvation has laid a foundation that allows us to build a whole lifestyle that shows we belong to God. In building a Christian testimony, it's only as we follow on in our understanding and enjoyment of grace that what affects us spiritually will also affect us practically. God's outpouring of grace is for our assistance in worship. We hear the evidence of this in every worship gathering, as brethren offer their appreciation of Christ, and God sees the same evidence in sisters as they silently offer theirs. We can say, like Barnabas, that we have seen the grace of God, and are glad (2).

Peter was a married man and his wife accompanied him in his work for the Lord (3). She was a believer, but this didn't mean that he was freed from the challenges that belong to a marriage where one isn't a believer. In his case, both he and his wife would demonstrate to one another the adorning that belongs to "the hidden person of the heart." In this way, they would thoroughly enjoy that they were *"heirs together of the grace of life"* and be thankful for the wide-ranging opportunities to share it with each other.

Back in the days of horse-drawn carriages in the mid-18th century, a man sat opposite a woman who was visibly moved by what she was reading. The man asked if she would show him what it was that affected her so much, and she passed him the book. He read:

"O to grace how great a debtor
Daily I'm constrained to be!
Let that grace, Lord, like a fetter,
Bind my wandering heart to Thee.
Prone to wander, Lord, I feel it,
Prone to leave the God I love;
Keep my heart from wandering, keep it
Till I'm perfected above."

The man reportedly handed the book back to her with the words, "Would to God that I were in the condition now that I was when I wrote these words!" He was Robert Robinson, the author of the hymn.

Many know what it is to turn aside temporarily from the Lord at some stage in their lives, and then look back on it with deep regret. Thankfully, the Lord graciously restores the years that the locusts have eaten, even when they have been destructively nibbling away inside a marriage. For some, this has been a real source of prayerful concern regarding their partnership, their family and home life.

Wives, Likewise

Chapter 2 ends with our eyes being fixed on *"the Shepherd and Overseer"* – the Pastor and Protector – *"of your souls,"* and chapter 3 begins with *"Wives."* Some versions say, *"Likewise"* or *"In the same way."* The original says *'Homoioōs hai gunaikes'* – which means, "Similarly the wives." Peter has a fitting way of making it clear to us that the One who is the cause of our worship also is the cause of our submission.

"Come with Thy light divine into each room to shine.
Master, the house is Thine, search Thou and see."

He has come right inside your house, and is longing to see that every-thing is consistent with your service in chapter 2 and with your salvation in chapter 1. We would think it strange if someone received a letter and had forgotten the contents of pages 1 and 2 by the time page 3 was being read. In exactly the same way, Peter wants us to see that chapter 2 is the doorway into the home in chapter 3. By saying, *"Likewise,"* he helps us to focus on the submissive spirit that causes us to worship, helps the effective witness of our walk, makes us live as good citizens before the authorities, and be the kind of workers that respect employers. It is Peter's way of saying that the marriage relationship has to be exactly the same, and for the same reasons.

Two thoughts should promote a desire to submit: i) to reflect our higher relationship with the Shepherd and Overseer of our souls and ii) to maintain a good relationship with others – authorities, employers, marriage partners.

It's as if God is knocking on the door of our homes to say *"Wives ... be submissive,"* but this doesn't always go down well in today's world, where feminism can resist any thought of submission. No sister should ever let it enter her mind that chauvinism and feminism have any place in God's order of divine service. No sister should ever feel that she is of secondary importance to God, for there's nothing degrading of women in His Word. There's a harmony of teaching where one complements the other, and there may not be the slightest difference between the value of what a sister gives and what comes from brethren. There are sisters who have served the Lord monumentally, and God knows all about it. He also knows your service, and it's not second-rate to your husbands, never for a moment.

Adornment

The wife who wins her husband must be winsome! But where does her winsomeness come from? Some women obviously believe it's from the appeal of outward glamour, but Peter identifies it as belonging to an inner glory. The word *kosmos* and its derivations is used one hundred and eighty-six times in the New Testament and is translated as "world" on every occasion except this one. God could hardly have given Christian women a higher or more elevated commendation. Since it normally refers to the order and beauty of His creation, to the evidence of His handiwork in the world, it's as if He says to our sisters, "I think the world of you."

Their adornment is of His making, and Peter applies it to how it becomes evident in the life of the believing wife. It's not standing in front of the mirror, but looking into the mirror of His Word. It's not the decorating of the outside, but the cultivation of the inside. It's not what she does externally for herself – an elaborate hairdo, decorating herself, or wearing the best dress in her wardrobe – but the ornamentation God produces internally that only believers can possess.

It's in a gracious way that this former rugged fisherman held out the positive beauty of the inner person that has been created in Christ. The new nature that shines in the meek and quiet spirit reflects what He is, and is like a shaft of light from Matthew 11:29 – *"I am gentle and lowly in heart."* It was the only time He ever spoke about His own heart, and He said it at a time when He invited others to unburden theirs. It was as if He were asking them to tell Him what was in their hearts that He could take, and He would tell them what is in His heart that they could take.

Husbands, Likewise

Having begun with *"Wives, likewise,"* Peter now balances his conversation by saying, *"Husbands, likewise."* There's an onus on both of them, and he wants the woman to understand that in the eyes of her husband, and of God, he's going to treat her as the weaker vessel. This means physically; not spiritually, mentally or emotionally. Husbands have to dwell with their wives *"with understanding."* This carries the thought of careful and caring investigation, and means having due consideration of her temperament, personality, outlook, strengths and weaknesses, abilities and deficiencies, and above all her spirituality. In this way, husbands will treat their wives as the Lord intends, and cause their whole family life to be exposed to His blessing.

Showing this depth of interest in each other's character is good and healthy, but it must always be accompanied by joint spiritual investigation of what God has for them as couples. There's a lovely presentation of this in Psalm 128. The husband is the expected breadwinner, and his wife is described as a fruitful vine in the innermost part of their house. To complete the picture, their children sit around the family table like olive plants, and you may wonder why?

God's description is in keeping with the rest of the teaching about olives in the Old Testament. Oil came from the olive, and from the oil came the light for the lampstand in the tabernacle, so there's a testimony round about that table that allowed Him to see the working of His Spirit. The oil was a symbol of Him, as Zechariah 4:2-6 helps us to understand, and it was this working that allowed God to see something in their house that resembled something that He saw and enjoyed in His. Let's have a look at how Peter shows how we can arrive at this kind of marital bond and what he presents as necessary in the lives of a couple who, by God's help, can help one another in the mutual enjoyment of *"the grace of life."*

The Word

Peter is still drawing on the value of chapter 2:2-3, and reasoning that a believer's first experience of the Word in the gospel will create the desire for more of it, including in marriage. It's good when couples have a readiness to share the Word with each other, for this means they are bringing the desire for the Word into their marriage. It's noticeable, however, that Peter doesn't assume that all husbands and wives are believers. This doesn't mean that he was advocating that a believer should marry an unbeliever; but rather that he was aware that the gospel had reached one, and not yet the other. He actually acknowledges that some will keep being disobedient by rejecting the Word spoken by their wives.

Without a Word

Now he foresees both kinds of marriages and advises wives, for example, to win their husbands through the appeal of their godly conduct. Her attitude and actions may allow what she shows to have more impact than what she says. She may feel as if she's walking a tightrope as she figures out when to speak and when not to speak. There may be times when words have an effect; but it's also quite likely there will be times when body language speaks more loudly than words. This doesn't mean, of course, that he can be saved "without the word," since it is the means God uses to bring every person to Christ. James makes it clear that it is *"of His own will He brought us forth by the word of truth"* (4) and Peter corroborated this in chapter 1:23 by saying we have *"been born again ... through the word of God which lives and abides forever."*

Her wisdom in this is combined with *"fear,"* which is the same word Paul used, and is translated by the New King James Version as *"that she respects her husband"* (5). Peter recognised that husbands would *"observe"* this and, to show that they'd be paying attention, he returned to the same word he used about how Gentiles would be watching and inspecting what believers did and what they didn't do (6). Failure on her part would come from not living up to what God expected from her, but, along with this, she could cause the Word of God to be blasphemed by being unwise (7). She had married a man, probably as two unbelievers; but now, as a believer, she was trying to win him. The reality is, she was no longer the person he married – her outlook was different, her character had changed – so Peter says it may be her behaviour that will talk. If so, the lesson is clear: let it do the talking when you know that you're unlikely to win him with words.

Heirs Together of the Grace of Life

The husband and wife, the stronger and weaker, never implies inequality, and Peter's way of confirming this is to emphasise their bond of equality as co-sharers, fellow-heirs of this particular expression of grace that God has reserved for marriage. This is of real importance, since God Himself was the Designer of marriage in the Garden of Eden. The woman He *"made"* (Heb. *banah*: built) was God's ideal for the first man Adam (8), and God brought her to Adam as a building, a body and a bride – as a foreshadowing of the Last Adam receiving *"the church, which is His body"* (9).

It's also important from the point of view of believers being united with their Saviour as *"joint heirs with Christ"* (10). The adversary will do his utmost to keep believers from communing with God. He did it in the Garden of Eden with the first couple, and he's still doing it. As individuals, we can let sin disrupt our fellowship with Him. On the other hand, we can make sure this doesn't happen. Couples should keep their eyes fixed on their spiritual inheritance and on all the blessings it allows them to share in the deepest possible way within marriage. As two whom the Lord has joined, they have the greatest and closest opportunity to enjoy the fruits of their salvation.

That Your Prayers May Not Be Hindered

As individuals, we can let sin disrupt our fellowship with Him. On the other hand, we can make sure this doesn't happen. The writer of Psalm 66:18-20 couldn't have been more straightforward when he said, *"If I regard iniquity in my heart, the Lord will not hear. But certainly God has heard me: He has attended to the voice of my prayer. Blessed be God, who has not turned away my prayer; nor His mercy from me!"* So there can be hindrances individually, and Peter indicates there can be marital hindrances. Both partners have been guided by the word *"Likewise,"* and lack of fulfilling their obligations to each other would "hinder" their prayers. Peter means that her lack of submission, his lack of understanding and care, or their joint lack of appreciation of being *"heirs together,"* would interfere or cut into their prayers being voiced by them or heard by God.

Finally, All of You

It's as if Peter is the expert fisherman in this chapter, and no one's getting off the hook! Having focused on wives and husbands, he now includes everyone: the singles as well as the married, the old as well as the young, and he has a sevenfold standard for all:

1. **Of one mind** (*Gr. homophrones: likeminded*) - harmony in assembly

life depends on everyone thinking the same.

2. **Compassion** *(Gr. sumpatheis: fellow-feeling)* - having a sensitivity for each other without being selective.

3. **Love as brothers** *(Gr. philadelphoi: fond of brethren)* - having genuine affection for one another without favour or disregard.

4. **Tender-hearted** *(Gr. eusplagchnoi: full of pity)* - having sensitivity to the hurts and pains of others.

5. **Courteous** *(Gr. tapeinofrones: humble-minded)* - having a Christlike lowly mind that takes account of everyone and being willing to serve all. This can be a challenge, and easily overlooked.

6. **Not returning evil** *(Gr. kakon: harm, injury)* - having no desire to retaliate or get even with wrong actions or words, remembering that insults can be as hurtful as blows. The Jews opposed Jeremiah and urged one another to *"attack him with the tongue"* (Jeremiah 18:18). No wonder James spoke so much about it (James .1:26; 3:5,6,8)!

7. **Blessing** *(Gr. eulogia: speak well of)* - having the desire to say something beneficial and praiseworthy that will be encouraging and uplifting.

These seven requirements form a vital part of our spiritual relationship with one another, and they form a vital part of God's reason for calling us to Himself, and for granting many the blessing of 'marital' grace.

(1) Ps.90:2 (2) Acts 11:23 (3) 1 Cor.9:5 (4) Jas.1:18 (5) Eph.5:33 (6) 1 Pet.2:12 (7) Tit.2:5 (8) 1 Cor.15:45 (9) Eph.1:22,23 (10) Rom.8:17

1 Peter 1:15-16 and 1 Peter 3:15-16

"*But as He who called you is holy, you also be holy in all your conduct, because it is written, 'Be holy, for I am holy'*" (1 Peter 1:15,16).

"*But sanctify in your hearts Christ as Lord,*" (RV*) "*and always be ready to give a defence to everyone who asks you a reason for the hope that is in you, with meekness and fear; having a good conscience, that when they defame you as evildoers, those who revile your good conduct in Christ may be ashamed*" (1 Peter 3:15,16, NKJV).

* see marginal footnote

7. GRACE RECOGNISED IN HOLINESS

It's impossible to make Christ what He already is. We can't make Him holy, nor can we make Him Lord for He already is holy, and He already is Lord. In eternity past, in His time on earth, and now on the throne of heaven, His holiness and lordship are without question and always intact.

So how do we sanctify Him as Lord? We cannot improve them in Him, but He can improve them in us. So what does Peter mean? The key to the question is *"in your hearts"*; He resides there, but does He preside? How do we know, and how can others tell? This is the experiential enthronement of our Saviour, not only as Purchaser but also as Proprietor of our lives. He is Lord, which means He is the Master; but if we say *"He is my Lord,"* this means the Master has the mastery. We can think of this in three ways:

- It affects Him - through having constant communion with Him
- It affects us - through His constant claims on the whole person
- It affects others - through communicating Christ to personal contacts

In each of those three areas of sanctification, the accent is on our being set apart in Him and for Him. In 1 Peter 3:15, the emphasis is on His being set apart in us. Peter's ten-point checklist is right here:

- Am I sufficiently growing in the Word? (1 Peter 2:2)
- Am I a thankful worshipper? (1 Peter 2:4,5)
- Am I an active witness? (1 Peter 2:9,10)
- Am I careful in my walk? (1 Peter 2:11,12)
- Am I submissive to worldly authorities? (1 Peter 2:13-17)
- Am I submissive at work? (1 Peter 2:18-20)
- Am I a submissive wife or husband? (1 Peter 3:1-6)
- Am I a blessing to others in the church? (1 Peter 3:8,9)
- Am I always ready to defend my hope? (1 Peter 3:15)
- Am I living with a clear conscience? (1 Peter 3:16)

How blessed we are that the crucified *"Lord of glory"* (1) and the exalted Lord who has been *"received up in glory"* (2) should want to be set apart in holiness in our hearts! Right at the outset, we acknowledge our unworthiness even to think or speak about something so lofty as the holiness of God. It's a very high privilege that He would allow our very limited minds to consider what He intrinsically is by nature, since He knows what we instinctively are in ours.

It's not only that His conduct is holy, He is holy; and it's not simply because there's an absence of sin in Him. When Pilate interrogated the Lord Jesus Christ, He wasn't proved holy because Pilate found no fault in Him; rather Pilate found no fault in Him because He is holy. As we delight in the privilege of stepping inside the precinct of the holiness of God, it towers above us causing us to sense our own sinfulness.

It's not that the absence of sinfulness in Him makes Him holy, it's that the presence of infinite holiness makes Him sinless. It wasn't only when He was on earth that He did no sin: the eternal truth is that *"in Him there is no sin"* (3). There is never a moment when He stepped out of *"being in the form of God"* (4). He is never less than eternally holy for He is eternally God!

James tells us that when we enter into a transaction that confirms our sinfulness, it's because the temptation conceives with the lust in our nature and produces sin (5). This was not the case with the Saviour. In His unique holiness, there is nothing in Him with which lust can conceive. There is a complete absence of anything in His nature that would allow temptation to become an inward thought, and therefore no possibility of a sinful outward action being produced. Some have said that He could have sinned, but didn't. The truth is that in absolute holiness He didn't sin, because He couldn't. He is the Holy One, Son of the holy God, and the Holy Spirit is called the Spirit of holiness (6).

It's not that holiness is a characteristic of Their joint-nature, just as light and love are not simply features of Their Being. It's what They are, and what They share. They are contrary to our human nature, yet They choose to share some of Their attributes through saving grace. This allows us to receive imputed holiness by which we can become holy in lifestyle, but They are not receivers of holiness, They are its sole Givers, but we possess none of it until we know His salvation.

The way Peter presents this in his letter is wonderfully consistent with what we have in the first reference to His holiness in the book of Exodus. After the Passover had taken place. God gave them a way out of Egypt by the blood of the lamb, and then a way through the Red Sea. In response, Moses and the people sang in triumph of the God who is *"glorious in holiness"* (7). When we go forward into Exodus 28, we read how God took them closer to Himself through a high priest with garments and a holy crown on his head that was engraved with the words *"Holiness to*

Jehovah" (8).

What they had acknowledged on the day of their deliverance God wanted them to acknowledge every day when, at last, they encamped around His dwelling place. What a huge step forward! Instead of being in bondage in the presence of the enemy, they had a man who expressed their freedom in the presence of God. When we move forward again, we find the third mention of God's holiness in 1 Chronicles 16:29 when His people were invited to *"worship the LORD in the beauty of holiness!"*

These are the first three references to holiness in our Bible and we can see how God was travelling and leading His people. He began with the redeemed; then showed that there was a man in His presence for them; and then He caused them to approach and worship Him in the beauty of holy array. This is exactly the order we see in 1 Peter 1 and 2. God begins with the work of the Redeemer and the Passover Lamb in chapter 1; He continues with the work of Christ the High Priest in chapter 2; and the rest of the letter continues with a theme that begins with the worship of the people of God in the presence of God through the Man who represents us there.

Isn't it amazing how consistent God is? He has an order in the Old Testament that foreshadows His order in the New Testament. His people were well blessed through Moses, yet we have much more in Christ. In His gracious desire to deliver His redeemed through Christ, God triply blesses us by allowing us to enter into His holiness. He brings us into the holiness of the Person, into the holiness of His purpose, and into the holiness of His Holy Place to worship Him.

Sanctification

When we come to the New Testament, the triumphs of our salvation are laid out for us in Acts 26:18 – *"to open their eyes, in order to turn them from darkness to light, and from the power of Satan to God, that they may receive forgiveness of sins and an inheritance among those who are sanctified by faith in Me."* This is the beginning of God's great work of sanctification in the believer right from the moment of salvation.

Sometimes our Bibles will tell us in a marginal note that being sanctified means being set apart; but it means much more. It's very easy to set someone or something apart, but this doesn't necessarily mean that they have been set apart in holiness. The word Paul used was *hagiazō*, which means "made holy," and it has to do with the character or condition in which we are set apart by God. The word sanctified belongs to the thought of holiness, so he's really saying we have been set apart in holiness for God.

This is how God begins, and Hebrews 10:8-10 takes us back to Calvary to show us that the mainstream of His holiness has been channelled through the work of the Saviour. It was there He fulfilled the will of God, and *"By that will we have been sanctified through the offering of the body of Jesus Christ once for all."* Out of Calvary's darkness, light has flooded our souls; and out of Calvary's sinfulness, holiness has been given to us through the cleansing power of His precious blood. No wonder the writer calls it *"So great a salvation"*! (9).

Paul tells us, in 1 Thessalonians 2:13, that we have come into the blessing of salvation *"through sanctification by the Spirit"* – that was His part; *"and belief in the truth"* – that was our part. Even in the very nature of our calling, God has made it clear that it is high, and holy, and heavenly

87

(10). What is God trying to tell us? Well, He wants us to know that our high calling refers to our station in Christ. We are seated with Him in the heavenly places (11). As far as our eternal welfare is concerned, He has covered us in His holiness, and this leaves the believer completely untouchable by the destructive power of the adversary. You are out of his reach, as far as your eternal welfare is concerned. He cannot snatch you out of your Saviour's hand (12). Our station is secure, but we have a standard to maintain, and there are two parts to it. Peter leaves us in no doubt that the station we have obtained in salvation has a standard that must be maintained and attained in our service.

He also moves on to show us that the calling, which is holy in its character, is also holy in its purpose. When God says, *"Be holy for I am holy,"* He combines His eternal name with His eternal character in the phrase *egō hagios eimi.* He is the holy I AM! This makes us partakers of the divine nature, but doesn't, of course, make us equal with Him. There's something in us that responds to the high calling, something in us that responds to the holiness of that calling, and something in us that responds to fulfilling the purpose of our heavenly calling. It's by fulfilling this that we experience the privilege and pleasure of the priestly service that Hebrews and 1 Peter speak about.

Sadly, religion has its counterfeit holiness, with its so-called holy places and holy men, yet there's nothing of the holiness of God in them - for unregenerate men can never be holy. History shows that some of the Caesars, including Julius Caesar and Augustus, had coins with an inscription that defied Deity. They claimed the title Pontifex Maximus, which in Latin means the greatest high priest. In the fifth century, it became a title of Popes and does to the present day.

When Pope Benedict was active, he had a new set of doors made for the

Vatican with his name and title inscribed across its four panels. It's a bold statement of Roman Catholic belief, which also claims the title of Holy Father and His Holiness. In the Upper Room, the Lord Jesus addressed God in prayer as "Holy Father," and He is the only One who rightly bears the Name. Similarly, the Lord Jesus Christ is the only great High Priest, yet Pontifex Maximus, the greatest high priest, claims to be two levels higher!

In marked contrast to all this, Peter introduces the personal holiness of believers in chapter 1, then he speaks about a holy priesthood and a holy nation in chapter 2 before urging us to set Christ apart in holiness in our hearts in chapter 3. How significant it is that the 'Holy I AM' calls us individually to live in His holy character, collectively to live in the holy atmosphere of assembly service, and then emphasises that we must live in the purity and authority of the holiness and lordship of His Person. Service is very important, but having the right environment for spiritual service makes it more important. We should notice how appropriate this is. He is asking us to give an answer to everyone who asks a reason for the hope that is in us, that we do it with meekness and fear.

It's not simply a matter of giving an answer. The character of the answerer is what matters. Without this, the answer will never be right. Well, it could be the right thing, but said in the wrong way. It needs to be a Christlike answer. In fact, in the last chapter, we saw it was possible for a wife to win her husband through silence that allows Christian character to speak; for there are times when conduct has a louder voice. So we need to take both chapters: one, to learn what to say in the right place; and, secondly, to learn what not to say in another place. We just need to see these two opportunities as ways in which the holiness of God can speak through each one of us.

This will enable us to fulfil two things: i) the silent witness of our manner of life (1 Peter 3:1) and ii) the verbal witness that's done in meekness and in fear (1 Pet.3:15). The Lord is *the Faithful and True Witness"* (13), whether silent or speaking, and we take character from Him.

> "Lord, speak to me, that I may speak
> In living echoes of Thy tone;
> As Thou hast sought, so let me seek
> Thine erring children, lost and lone."
> (Frances R. Havergal)

Holiness is the best preparation for enabling us to walk with God and fulfilling the kind of ministry that Peter is outlining to us. Paul wholeheartedly agrees, and his message to Timothy is as vital for us: *"Therefore if anyone cleanses himself from the latter, he will be a vessel for honour, sanctified and useful for the Master, prepared for every good work"* (14). This means leaving things behind, and going after the things that are before, so there's an essential combination: *"depart from iniquity"* (15) and *"Pursue peace with all people, and holiness, without which no man will see the Lord"* (16). Forsake sinfulness, and follow holiness. What a goal! What an ambition, to have the holiness of God before us always and to be thinking about the possibility of our lives reflecting the very nature of our God.

We have been emphasising how everything in chapter two and onwards goes back to desiring the pure milk of the Word, and it's vital that we do this in the matter of knowing when to speak and when not to speak. Solomon's advice was that there's *"a time to keep silence, and a time to speak"* (17). This is what Peter is saying, too, but now he's asking us to take on board that holiness must be harnessed to the Word.

It's beneficial to follow his reasoning: in chapter 1, *"Be holy, for I am holy"*; in chapter 2, *"desire the pure milk of the word."* You see, it's not enough to use the Word without the spiritual back-up of the holiness of God. Speaking the Word without holiness being our motivation will make the Word powerless through us. It's important to come to our Bible and recognise it as the Holy Word of God, written by men who spoke from Him as they were moved by the Holy Spirit. When we recognise the holiness from which the inspired Word has come, we have a responsibility to pass it on in a similar way. It has to be communicated in holiness through the sanctified vessel.

So we go back through everything we have been thinking about and we discover the need to ask, once again, are we growing in the Word? We can add to this by asking if our desire for holiness is causing us to grow in the Word? And is our desire for the Word causing us to grow in holiness? Both should happen, shouldn't they? The Word will help us to grow in holiness, but the initial desire for the Word will come from your enjoyment of the holiness of God. The One who has spoken to us, in the first place, wants to speak through us, so that others might hear and see Him.

Partakers

Ever since Eden's Fall, God has desired fellowship with men and women on earth, and the chequered journey from Genesis to Malachi reveals the ups and downs of maintaining it. These were long years, during which the unchanging God was served, challenged and tested, by changeable individuals and a very unreliable people. There was failure among leaders, prophets, priests, kings, and tribes, yet the omniscient God who knows the end from the beginning never failed them. He held true to His promise that He would lead them into the land as victors over opposing nations, and His reliable assurance was based on this: *"God has spoken in His holiness"* (18).

When an unfaithful people forsook His law, He remained faithful. When they failed to show love to Him, His lovingkindness remained, and His whole promise was securely wrapped in this, *"Once I have sworn by My holiness"* (19). Holiness makes it impossible for God to lie or mislead, and His faithfulness is eternally rooted in His unchanging holiness.

Even at the place of the altar's intended close communion, the God-given mandate of *"Holiness to the LORD"* on the high priest's golden crown was no guarantee against inappropriate or unacceptable sacrifice in the days of Malachi (20). It was the place where proper sacrifice permitted those who offered to eat of the sacrifices as partakers of the altar (21), yet they lost the joy of sharing in holy things. This is how the Old Testament closes, on a note that holds a salutary warning, lest we should fail in the same way and lose our joy in holy things. God was patiently waiting for the opportunity to be given to us through the coming of His Son.

At last, the perfect Servant, the perfect Sacrifice, the perfect Saviour, and through Him perfect salvation! The gospel of Christ has come, and all things are ours *"according to the glorious gospel of the blessed* [happy] *God"* (22). With the gospel of Christ comes God's *"promise in Christ,"* and of this promise we have been made *"partakers"* (23). And what fellowship it is! The wealth of this verse increases when it is translated (as in the Revised Version) as, *"the Gentiles are fellow-heirs, and fellow-members of the body, and fellow-partakers of the promise in Christ Jesus through the gospel."* It's a threefold fellowship that links us, outwardly, with believers throughout the world; with the closest inseparable bond, inwardly, that we are in Christ; and have joint-fellowship in this glorious promise that points us, upwardly, to Him.

Paul uses three words – *sungkleeronoma ... sussēma ... summetocha* – and each one is an adjective to describe what Gentiles have, as well as believing Jews, in Christ. All three words begin with the prefix *sun*, which means union, togetherness and companionship, and Paul definitely enjoyed what God asked him to share. It was as if his heart was so full that no one word could capture the full extent of the blessing, and so his final word is rather special. On its own, the word *metochos* means a sharer or a partner. Adding the little word *sun* expands the thought of union and togetherness, and it allows the whole word to be something like "sharing-sharers" or "fellow-fellowshippers." We catch the sense of his enjoyment as he describes the gospel as "the unsearchable riches of Christ" in verse 8.

In Philippians, we are partakers of grace; in Hebrews, partakers of Christ and partakers of His holiness; and in Peter's second letter, we are partakers of the divine nature (24). Our fellowship, participation and sharing knows no bounds. God's grace, holiness and nature are for sharing, and although we are brought into them through the gospel, we grow in them by being on-going partakers. Peter indicates there are two sides to this: on the one hand, it's by taking and trusting God's promises; and on the other, it's because we have escaped the corruption that is in the world.

The pleasures of sin have gone; the pleasure of holiness has come. Our nature has changed. The old things have gone; what is new has come (25). We think differently, we speak differently, and we act differently, for we are presenting our bodies as living sacrifices that are holy (26), and this holiness, in contrast to the sub-standard offerings in Malachi's day, makes us acceptable in our service for the Lord. God sees Himself in Christ, and He wants to see Christ in us, for only then will His grace be recognised in holiness.

> "Where no stain of sin can enter, nor the gold be dim;
> In that holiness unsullied, I shall walk with Him;
> Meet companion for the Master, from Him, for Him made;
> Glory of God's grace for ever, there in me displayed."
> (Mrs Bevan)

There's quite a bit of parallelism in Peter's letter. He has done it with the word *"likewise"* in verses 1 and 7, and again by contrasting *"evildoers"* and *"good"* in verse 16, just as he did in verses 12 and 14 of the previous chapter. Another pairing is in verses 14 and 18 – *"if you should suffer"* and *"Christ also suffered"*; what an honour for these to be combined!

- Those who believe suffering on behalf of Christ
- Christ suffering on behalf of those who believe

Put to Death ... But Made Alive

The next couplet is not so easily explained. Bible scholars give different interpretations, and we understand why this is the case. Verse 18 says that Christ was put to death in the flesh but made alive in or by the Spirit. Translators also have difficulty, because the Greek language doesn't show if *spirit* should have a capital 'S' or be in the lower case. This has led to some being of the mind that He was made alive by the Holy Spirit, while others take the view that it was by His Own inner spirit.

Irrespective of viewpoint, all agree that He was *"put to death in the flesh"* by the work of men, but was *"made alive in the spirit"* by the work of God. Having said that, there are a couple of points worth considering.

This doesn't refer to His bodily resurrection, for He went while His body was in the tomb, during which time His own spirit was alive. His spirit never died with His body on the cross, and He had committed it into the safekeeping of His Father's hands (27).

He Went and Preached to the Spirits in Prison

Peter used the word *"preached"* four times in this letter. In 1 Peter 1:12, 25 and 1 Peter 4:6 he used the Greek word *euangelizō*, which means "evangelise," and it's only in 1 Peter 3:19 that *kerussō* is used. It simply means to herald a public proclamation, and by not using *euangelizō* he ruled out any thought of the Lord preaching the gospel to the lost, which would have made it the gospel of the second chance. By changing to *kērussō*, he indicated in vv.18-19 that He went there to make a triumphant statement of His victory on the cross. His victorious spirit made a victorious announcement to vanquished spirits.

Baptism ... the Answer of a Good Conscience

When Philip helped the Ethiopian eunuch to understand Isaiah 53:7-8, he preached to him in such a way that he saw his need to believe in Christ and then demonstrate his obedience by being baptised. Peter's message on the Day of Pentecost had the same effect. *Those who "accepted his message were baptised"* (28); so, just as with the Ethiopian, they understood the close connection between salvation and baptism. There was no long time gap between receiving and following. Conversion and commitment went hand in hand, as indicated in the implied sequence of death, burial and resurrection.

It's very much in keeping with the Lord's sufferings, as we read in chapters 2:21 and 3:18 that He said of them, *"I have a baptism to be baptised with"* (29). How well He knew that His deep suffering on the cross, particularly during the three hours of darkness, would be a complete immersion as God *"made Him who knew no sin to be sin for us"* (30). Like the ark being buffeted as it took the full force of the deluge, the Saviour was uniquely qualified to say to His Father, *"All Your waves and billows have gone over Me"* (31) and *"Your wrath lies heavy upon Me, and You have afflicted Me with all Your waves."* God held nothing back. For this reason, Paul was able to write, *"He who did not spare His own Son"* (32) meaning that God did not treat Him leniently.

Through the Resurrection of Jesus Christ

It's worth noting the specific relationship between Noah's ark and the Lord's resurrection. When the deluge was over, and God's work of deliverance and judgment finished, Genesis 8:4 says, *"Then the ark rested in the seventh month, the seventeenth day of the month."* This is significant. The seventh month in Genesis became the first month in Exodus 12:2 when God introduced the Passover. The lamb was slain on the 14th day, which foreshadowed the day of the Lord's crucifixion, and therefore, three days later, the 17th pointed forward to His resurrection.

Not the Removal of the Filth of the Flesh

Cleansing of sin is provided only through the precious blood of our Lord Jesus Christ. It alone is the price of propitiation (33), which satisfies a holy God and appeases His wrath while, at the same time, it *"cleanses us from all sin"* (34). So baptism is *"not the removal of the filth of the flesh."* Peter says it is *"the answer* [Gr. *eperōtēma:* the pledge, the inquiry] *of a good conscience."* Baptism asks questions, and then finds the answer in the genuine work that has been done in believers' hearts, which qualifies them to be baptised. It asks, like the Ethiopian, *"What hinders me from being baptised?" Conscience* and the heart replies, "Nothing!" The Lord went through a baptism of judgment that we might follow Him in a baptism of blessing. Can we, in all *"good conscience,"* say "No"? Instead, we say "Yes," because *"the love of Christ compels us"* (35), and because it's a step in sanctifying Christ as Lord in our hearts.

Angels and Authorities and Powers Having Been Made Subject to Him

The chapter begins with submissive wives, and it ends with submissive angels. Such is the triumph of the cross that sinful human beings and all sinless angelic beings bow before the supremacy of the resurrected Saviour (36), and those fallen angels who heard the Victor herald His conquest on the cross bow in submissive defeat.

> "Yonder throne for Him erected, now becomes the Victor's seat,
> Lo, the Man on earth rejected, angels worship at His feet!
> Day and night they cry before Him, 'Holy, holy, holy Lord,'
> All the powers of heaven adore Him, all obey His sovereign word."
> (T. Kelly)

(1) 1 Cor.2:8 (2) 1 Tim.3:16 (3) 1 Jn 3:5 (4) Phil.2:6 (5) Jas.1:15 (6) Rom.1:4; Josh.24:19; Lk.1:35 (7) Ex.15:11 (8) Ex.28:36, see also Isa.23:18, ASV (9) Heb.2:3 (10) Phil.3:14, KJV; 2 Tim.1:9; Heb.3:1 (11) Eph.2:6 (12) Jn 10:28,29 (13) Rev.3:14 (14) 2 Tim.2:21 (15) 2 Tim.2:19 (16) Heb.12:14 (17) Ecc.3:7 (18) Ps.60:6 (19) Ps.89:35 (20) Mal.1:7-14 (21) 1 Cor.10:18 (22) 1 Tim.1:11 (23) Eph.3:6 (24) Phil.1:7; Heb.3:14; 12:10; 2 Pet.1:4 (25) 2 Cor.5:17 (26) Rom.12:1 (27) Lk.23:46 (28) Acts 2:41 (29) Lk.12:50 (30) 2 Cor.5:21 (31) Ps.42:7; 88:7 (32) Rom.8:32 (33) Rom.3:25 (34) 1 Jn 1:7 (35) 2 Cor.5:14 (36) Eph.3:10,11

1 Peter 4:10-11

"As each one has received a gift, minister it to one another, as good stewards of the manifold grace of God. If anyone speaks, let him speak as the oracles of God. If anyone ministers, let him do it as with the ability which God supplies, that in all things God may be glorified through Jesus Christ, to whom belong the glory and the dominion forever and ever. Amen" (1 Peter 4:10,11).

8. GRACE REVEALED IN SPIRITUAL GIFTS

Like a jewel in its setting, Peter embeds three sentences that radiate thoughts of the glory of God and of His being glorified, and it's noticeable what lies on either side. On the one hand, he draws our attention to the sufferings of Christ and, on the other, to the sufferings of the Christian. It's as if he wants to remind us of the cost and of the consequences of spiritual gifts. They are traceable to the lowly mind of the suffering Saviour, and it should be evident in all our service that we arm ourselves with the same mind. Our will must be His will, just as His will was God's will (1); and our use of spiritual gifts must show a mindset that bears His lowliness.

It was through what He fulfilled in that lowly mind that His glory followed, and it was out of that glory that He *"gave gifts to men"* (2). Through the glorified Christ, He set the members in the body according to His pleasure (3), and it's also for his pleasure that we want to glorify Him through the gifts. So, just as the gifts flow from His sufferings and glory, we serve with them knowing that, even if suffering is ours, the glory will always flow back to Him.

Peter's references to the Lord's sufferings are significant from this point of view, that he uses two different words to describe them. In 1 Peter 1:11, he considers the hardship and pain of His afflictions, and we recognise right away that our word "pathos" lies at the heart of the Greek word *pathēma*. This word never left Peter, and we find it again in 1 Peter 5:1 where he says that he was *"a witness of the sufferings of Christ."* In both verses, he indicates the severity of the Saviour's sufferings by using the word in its plural form, *pathēmata*. Between these two verses, Peter follows the theme of the sufferings of Christ, but in chapters 2, 3 and 4, the word he uses is *paschō*.

Both words combine to tell of the physical and spiritual sufferings He endured: the first, includes the brutality from the hands of men; the second, focuses on the deeper suffering endured from the hand of God when *"He made Him who knew no sin to be sin for us"* (4), our sin-bearer and sin offering. In 1 Peter 2:21, He suffered to be our Example; in 1 Peter 3:18, He is the Just dying for the unjust; and in 1 Peter 4:1, He is the Servant who pleased His God (5). Peter speaks very tenderly about the sufferings of his Saviour, and he does it in a way that was very personal to him. There's no doubt that he would wish his readers, in his days and ours, to think as tenderly and personally as he did.

Now that he is speaking to us about the blessing of spiritual gifts, he makes it clear that unless we have an appreciation of His sufferings – His hardship and pain, and feel the passion of Christ – then these things will register rather low on our scale. They were much higher on Peter's, and they will have to be high on ours, too, as we try to fulfill our worship, our witness, our walk, and as wives before their husbands. So this is the setting within which he wants us to think about the manifestation of the grace of God that we could call ...

PENTECOSTAL

We were thinking in chapter 1 of grace that's eternal and sacrificial; then we thought of grace that is experimental in chapter 2, by which we prove our experience in the Word of God. It's only through this kind of scriptural experience that we prove that God's Word actually works in our lives. Chapter 3 applies grace to the marital bond; and chapter 4 goes on to speak about *"manifold grace,"* which we trace to the Day of Pentecost when the initial distribution of the gifts took place in the coming of the Holy Spirit.

Manifold Grace

The marvel is that God has never missed out a single person who ever came to Christ, all of them without exception being sharers in the diversity of spiritual gifts. It's this variety that Peter says is *"manifold."* It is multi-faceted and variegated, one complementing the other as mutual expressions of grace. In every New Testament reference to spiritual gifts, God provides for *"each one,"* so it's impossible to miss the point. Paul says it in Romans, Corinthians and Ephesians, and Peter does the same (6).

When he heard what Paul had written, he must have rejoiced in knowing that the Spirit of God had told him exactly the same thing, that each of us is gifted. This means that each one of us has a ministry, and it's up to us to make sure that we carry 1 Peter 2:2 with us. Peter encourages us that we should *"desire the pure milk of the word,"* knowing that it feeds our worship in chapter 2, fills our walk in chapter 3, and fuels the witness of our gifts in chapter 4. The truth is we can't worship without it, we can't walk without it, and we can't witness without it.

No gift can function without the Word, so it's vital that we avoid a low-burn lifestyle by spending time in it. If we gather the fuel, God will provide the fire! If He has called you to teach, expound the Word. If you are a preacher, preach the Word. If you are an encourager, use the Word. If you are among the helps, support others with the Word. Whatever He asks you to do, do it. *"Take heed to the ministry which you have received in the Lord, that you may fulfil it"* (7), but never attempt it without immersing yourself in the Word. We need to learn the secret of bowing before God and asking Him, *"Please, God, help me to know my role from Your Word."* As He feeds you with it, ask for His help in passing it on and, as He does this, gradually He will confirm your gift.

Good Stewards

Assembly life is the place He has given for our gifts to be exercised. Look around the disciples in your church and two things should come to mind: you are surrounded by that amount of gift, and each of you has to acknowledge that you have received a gift and *"minister it to one another, as good stewards of the manifold grace of God."* This combination is presented in each chapter that deals with spiritual gifts:

- Romans 12: To each one (v.3) - members of one another (v.5)
- 1 Corinthians 12: To each one (v.7) - the same care for one another (v.25, NASB)
- Ephesians 4: To each one (v.7) - bearing with one another (v.2)
- 1 Peter 4: As each one (verse 10) - minister it to one another (v.10)

By doing this, Paul says each one of us will be *"for the profit of all,"* (8) so we should be able to help in the recognition of gift - but how often have we been aware of this happening? Think of the Saviour's ministry. When He spoke to someone, did they profit? When He touched someone, did they profit? In His reaching out, whether speaking or serving, did others profit? For many, the answer was "Yes." It should be like this for us, too; but those who speak, Peter says, let (them) speak *"as utterances from God"* (NKJV margin). And those who serve, let them *"do it as with the ability that God supplies."* It's not the person's ability, but God's, and He is the only One who can supply it, which means He alone choreographs the working of the gifts.

Each church has to consider the Giver rather than the gifted, since He is the source and supplier. We fulfil our ministry and get fulfilment from it only when we are in tune with the triune God. This is made very clear in 1 Corinthians 12. There are diversities of gifts, but the same Spirit. There are differences of ministries, but the same Lord. And there are diversities of activities, but it is the same God who works all in all. There are differences in the gifts, ministries and activities, but they own the same Spirit, Lord, and God.

The gifts (Gr. *charismata*) are expressions of variegated grace; the ministries (Gr. *diakoniōn*) present various ways of serving; and activities (Gr. *energēmatōn*). No matter which aspect of spiritual gifts we possess, we own them with thankfulness to the Giver, and we take the lowly place as speakers, servants and stewards. This will ensure that our relationship with God and one another is right, and that our stewardship from God and toward one another is right, too.

Opportunity and responsibility go together, just as how we serve must always be coupled to where we serve. The local assembly is the initial sphere of service, and should be the place where individual responsibility finds encouragement from the church's collective responsibility, and from its leaders. Stewardship puts everyone on the same footing, for it means we all share in the caring management and overall function of the gifts to the glory of God and the assembly's good.

The inference is, of course, that we can be poor stewards. Manifold grace can be abused, just as grace can be. Paul knew well that some took advantage of God's free grace by thinking that, if grace allows you to be forgiven for sin, then the more you sin the more grace you will get. That's why he asked, in Romans 6:1, *"Shall we continue in sin that grace may abound?"* and immediately answered, *"Certainly not! How shall we who died to sin live any longer in it?"* Peter wants to safeguard us from the possible abuse of God's manifold grace, either by our gifts malfunctioning or not functioning at all.

Paul is a superb example of how we can be good stewards. In 1 Corinthians 4:1, he wanted others to see him as a servant of Christ, and he used a very unusual illustration. His choice of word was *hupēretēs*, to let them know that he was like an under-oarsmen way down low in the galley that probably had three tiers of oarsmen with him in the bottom level. In that lowly frame of mind, he added, *"and steward[s] of the mysteries of God."* That would make anyone row well, wouldn't it? What an exalted place for a lowly man! Sometimes, if we are being honest with ourselves, we struggle in our rowing. There was a time when Jesus saw His disciples *"toiling in rowing"* (9), as He watched over them from His mountain place of prayer in the fourth watch of the night. Somewhere between three and six o'clock in the morning, in the last watch before dawn, they saw Him coming. It's such a graphic picture of us, isn't it? It's just before the dawning of the morning of that great and glorious day, and maybe we are toiling as we row.

"Oft we tread the path before us, with a weary, burdened heart;
Oft we toil amid the shadows, and our fields are far apart;
But the Saviour's "Come, ye blessed" all our labour will repay,

When we gather in the morning, where the mists have rolled away."

(Annie Herbert)

Unlike the disciples, Paul's lowly mind was on higher things, but this didn't make him high-minded. Listen to him, as he appeals to us from his lowly way of thinking: *"I say, through the grace given to me, to everyone who is among you, not to think of himself more highly than he ought to think, but to think soberly, as God has dealt to each one a measure of faith"* (10). There's always a danger that being gifted makes us think in ways we shouldn't. Our minds can shoot off into areas where we shouldn't be, and we assume that somehow or other the gifts reflect well on the individual who might be gifted. But it's all about the Giver, not the gift, and not the gifted. We must speak and serve as good stewards!

Neither Male Nor Female

When we are thinking of the distribution of spiritual gifts, it's important that we take in the implications of what Paul wrote in Galatians 3:28 – *"There is neither Jew nor Greek, there is neither slave nor free, there is neither male nor female; for you are all one in Christ Jesus."* Culture, class and gender are completely overcome, so we know right away that the redeemed among Jews are as equally gifted as Gentiles. Born-again slaves are equally blessed as their free counterparts, and no distinction exists between males and females in the distribution of the gifts. All these natural differences are removed in the church, which is the body of Christ, and all believers are members of one another (11).

In all this equality, it's just as likely that a sister will be a teacher, as a brother; it's just as likely that she will be an evangelist, as a brother; and pastoral tendencies will be just as evident in some sisters, as they are in some brethren. The same applies throughout the range of the gifts:

her gift may be identical, but a difference will be seen in her sphere of service. This doesn't imply inequality or inferiority, simply that God has determined that her role is different. He has arranged that women should *"learn in silence with all submission,"* so they receive the same teaching as their brethren, even though they are not permitted to teach publicly in the church (12). However, other opportunities are open to them, so that they can fulfil a speaking or written ministry, including one of teaching or encouraging.

In fact, older women are expected to be *"teachers of good things"* (13) (Gr. *Kalodidaskalos*) so this is one example of a God-given sphere, and there are others such as youth work and camps, and in missionary work. Some sisters have shown teaching ability in their letters to those who are going through difficult times, and their spiritual perception is well known. There are many ways of teaching, witnessing and encouraging, and God will always make sure that those He feeds are never without outlets for their gifts.

After listening to a message about spiritual gifts, a dear old sister was heard saying, "You're not trying to tell us that sisters are gifted, are you?" Yes, sisters, you are gifted. Your way of presenting His Word may be different, but doesn't this also happen among your brethren? Not all of them teach in the same way. They all teach from the same Book, many are gifted in Bible Class situations; others are able writers, but don't have a freedom in public preaching or teaching; and still others are called to share in a platform ministry. The vital thing is that brothers and sisters are led by the Spirit of God to share the Word of God with fellow-believers, relatives, friends and neighbours.

Romans 16 is a wonderful example of sisters' gift. Right from its opening verse, we are introduced to Phoebe, who evidently was as bright as her name implies, and her brightness shone as a sister, a servant and as a supporter of many, including Paul. Then we meet Priscilla and Aquila, a wife and husband, renowned as Paul's fellow-workers and as teachers who helped to equip Apollos in *"the way of God more accurately"* (14). A whole list follows, including Tryphena and Tryphosa who, even though their names mean Dainty and Delicate, wore themselves out in the Lord. Each generation has its sisters who are of great practical help in many ways, but all should know that God has called and gifted you for a spiritual role among His people.

Foot ... Hand ... Ear ... Eye

If ever there was any difficulty about identifying gift in an assembly, Paul helps us in 1 Corinthians 12 to accept that they ought to be recognisable. By illustrating the connections of the human body, he shows the interaction of spiritual gifts in the local assembly, as its character reflects the church, which is the body of Christ (15). None is isolated from the other, and none is invited to think of itself as being of lesser value. For instance, the foot should never say it's of lesser value than a hand, nor should the ear ever say it's inferior to the eye. We are not graded in a way that makes anyone more important or less important. All that matters is that an aspect of Christ is being fulfilled in you.

Paul's reasoning seems to be that, just as the members are recognisable in the physical body – we know what a foot looks like, what a hand looks like, and what they do – therefore we should know what a teacher looks like. We should know what an evangelist sounds like and we should know who fills the role of a helper or one of administrations by what they do in the service of God.

Just as He Pleased

God's pleasure should be our highest motivation, our greatest obligation, and our deepest satisfaction. His choice of us, and purpose in us, is *"according to the good pleasure of His will"* (16). That is how our spiritual journey began, and it will end at the coming of the Lord when He gives each of us a body *"as He pleases"* (17). As for the present, Paul says that our setting *"in the body"* is *"just as He pleased"* (18) so we need to see what His objective is in the spiritual gifts.

This should prompt each one of us to ask some serious questions. Should my own body be for His pleasure? Should my assembly, as a small reflection of the church, which is His body, be for His pleasure? Yes, but can we know how? Again, the answer is "Yes." In the context of Romans 12, can I fulfil my gift and not fulfill verses 1 and 2? Or can I fulfill these verses and not fulfill my gift? Now the obvious answer is "No." There's real value in seeing why gifts are included in chapter 12, and not in one of the other chapters, for they are integral to the holiness and acceptability of presenting our bodes as a living sacrifice. God's pleasure rests on you and your service being laid on the altar as a sacrifice to Him, and in you fulfilling the first two verses by fulfilling the next five.

It's similar in 1 Corinthians 12. Can I serve my Lord and Master in an assembly without fulfilling my place in the church, which is His body? Is it possible that an assembly can profit without us fulfilling our gifts? In this chapter, God leaves us in no doubt that His saints profit through the ministry of the gifts and, for this reason, it's vital that a combination of gifts provides what each brother and sister doesn't possess. Our bodies are wonderful examples of the interdependent unity in the church, which is His body, and God purposefully transfers this image to the local assembly and says of its character, *"Now you are the body of Christ"* (19).

More questions arise when we look into Ephesians chapter 4. Verse 12 alerts us to the fact that our gifts are *"for the equipping of the saints for the work of ministry, for the edifying of the body of Christ."* There are evangelists, pastors and teachers, and other gifts besides, but the real test of our ministry is in knowing how it is equipping the saints. How is our ministry helping to build up the church, which is the body of Christ? We say to all our brothers and sisters that if your ministry helps the work of someone else, and their input helps you, then our mutual care for each other brings us to what Peter has written. His aim is *"that in all things God may be glorified."*

Is it possible fully to do this without the God-honouring service of the gifts? On a personal level, we ask, "Can I really glorify God without fulfilling my gift?" Well, we can glorify God in our prayer lives; we can glorify Him by desiring to be Christ-like, and by growing in the grace and knowledge of our Lord Jesus Christ (2 Peter 3:18). All this will glorify God, but Peter encourages us to make sure we also glorify Him in the use of our gift.

A Man's Gift

Before rounding off this chapter, it may be worthwhile looking at an often-quoted verse from the Old Testament book of Proverbs, which says, *"A man's gift makes room for him, and brings him before great men"* (20). Some have used this to suggest that a brother's spiritual gift will overcome his timidity and bring him to the foreground of spiritual service. God certainly will enable those whom He calls, but this is not what Solomon had in mind. He was thinking about a bribe, some would call it a backhander, which causes some to turn a blind eye to an offence and makes the offender accepted.

Spiritual gifts belong to the New Testament teaching of the church, which is the body of Christ, and, of course, nothing of this was known in Solomon's day. So, whenever you hear this particular verse cited in the matter of spiritual gifts, you know it really doesn't apply, Even so, there's plenty to encourage you in the New Testament of your Bible, and God is waiting for you, even if it's only to fill a little space and Christ being glorified.

Father, Where Shall I Work Today?

"Father, where shall I work today?
And my love flowed warm and free
And he pointed me out a tiny spot
And he said, "Tend that for Me."
I answered quickly, "Oh no, not that!
Why, no one would ever see
However well the work was done,
Not that little place for me."
The word he spoke, it was not stern,
He answered me tenderly:
"Ah, little one, search that heart of thine,
Are you working for them or for Me?
Nazareth was just a little place, so was Galilee."
(Meade MacGuire)

(1) 1 Pet.4:1,2 (2) Eph.4:8 (3) 1 Cor.12:18 (4) 2 Cor.5:21 (5) Isa.53:10,11 (6) Rom.12:3; 1 Cor.12:11; Eph.4:7; 1 Pet.4:10 (7) Col.4:17 (8) 1 Cor.12:7 (9) Mk.6:48, KJV (10) Rom.12:3 (11) Rom.12:5 (12) 1 Tim.2:11,12 (13) Tit.2:3 (14) Acts 18:24-25 (15) Eph.1:22,23 (16) Eph.1:4,5 (17) 1 Cor.15:38 (18) 1 Cor.12:18 (19) 1 Cor.12:27 (20) Prov.18:16

1 Peter 5:1-7

"The elders who are among you I exhort, I who am a fellow elder and a witness of the sufferings of Christ, and also a partaker of the glory that will be revealed: shepherd the flock of God which is among you, serving as overseers, not by compulsion but willingly, not for dishonest gain but eagerly; nor as being lords over those entrusted to you, but being examples to the flock; and when the Chief Shepherd appears, you will receive the crown of glory that does not fade away.

Likewise you younger people, submit yourselves to your elders. Yes, all of you be submissive to one another, and be clothed with humility, for 'God resists the proud, but gives grace to the humble.' Therefore humble yourselves under the mighty hand of God, that He may exalt you in due time, casting all your care upon Him, for He cares for you" (1 Peter 5:1-7).

9. GRACE REFLECTED IN LEADERSHIP

To Peter, grace is a kaleidoscope. It has been conveniently packaged into a one-size-fits-all GRACE acrostic – God's Riches At Christ's Expense – which suits our modern liking for soundbites, but it doesn't quite capture Peter's thinking. His own word, *"manifold,"* is colourful in itself, yet it describes only one aspect of God's riches regarding spiritual gifts. To him, their spectrum of usefulness in service is like a range of heavenly iridescent colour, like aurora borealis or aurora australis, yet much more. He sees the nature of God, resplendent in Christ, in each chapter with all their colours blending: it's eternal, sacrificial, experimental, marital, Pentecostal, and now a new colour comes into the mix, for it is pastoral.

Left to ourselves, we might struggle to equate or define leadership with grace, but how graciously Peter does it for us! In its earlier expressions, in chapter 1 it's evidently for everyone who owns God's salvation; then it's for all who engage in spiritual service, brothers and sisters alike. Moving into chapter 3, it's for wives and husbands, as a beautiful reflection of *"Husbands, love your wives, just as Christ also loved the church and gave Himself for her"* (1). But, even here, it is extended to *"all of you"* in its wide-ranging aspects of care. The beauty of chapter 4's array of gift is that no one is missed out. Without exception, every believer is included. Then we step into chapter 5, and there seems to be a sudden change, but is there?

PASTORAL GRACE

There's no doubt whatsoever that Peter is speaking to a group within a much larger group – *"the elders who are among you"* – so it's not everyone who is called to share in the work of overseers among the gatherings of the Lord's people, yet all are called to relate to them in their work. We are called to be supportive of them, to a sense of a common understanding and mutual appreciation. It's with a deep sense of God and His will that, just as they fulfil their responsibilities as overseers, so also does the flock. So, as we think about pastoral grace, we want to see it from both sides. We are looking at brethren who are called by God to be overseers and to the rest of us who are called within the range of assembly service to acknowledge that their responsibility to Him and the flock needs to be reflected in our responsibility to Him and to them.

Some versions begin 1 Peter 5:1 by saying, *"Therefore"* or *"So,"* which links it directly to what has been said before and translates *presbuterous oun* as *"Elders therefore."* As we read the end of chapter 4, we may wonder why Peter didn't introduce his message to the elders at the beginning of chapter 3, when he had just referred to the Lord Jesus Christ as *"the Shepherd and Overseer of your souls."* He must have expected these dear brethren to trace his reasoning farther back than the thought of Christians suffering in 1 Peter 4:19 to the sufferings of Christ in 1 Peter 2:21-25.

We were thinking of how Peter has gone very carefully from the grace that was required in the man to the grace that was restored in his mistakes, and these remind us of our own need for remedial grace. Overseers are not exempt from being under the umbrella of requiring grace, or of needing times of restoring and uplifting grace. They must never lose their sense of all the aspects of grace that have come through the gospel, because we can't lose these and keep our understanding of the sheep. Missing out in our relationship with the Shepherd and Overseer of our souls will guarantee that we miss out in our relationship with His flock.

Elders are among the flock. In some ways it's true that they are over the sheep (2), but time after time the apostles, both Paul and Peter, use the word *"among"* (3). When Peter thought about overseers in all five regions, he was pointing out to the assemblies that these men know what you are going through. They are in it with you. They are among you, not at a distance from you. The Shepherd must never be far from his sheep. In much of a shepherd's work on a farm, practically speaking, he's within hands reach of his sheep. If this is true in the physical realm, it's equally true in the spiritual. If we don't live in a close relationship with the sheep there will be greater difficulty in assisting them in their times of need.

'Among the flock' means being in touch. These men faced the same circumstances. Their struggles were the same, for they also lived as foreign residents in a country that wasn't theirs. They'd been dispersed throughout this region and as total strangers they were spiritual pilgrims who had to make the best of it. God had put them there and in His sovereignty had a reason for doing so: He would be glorified, even on the basis of this one condition, that pastoral grace would be appreciated among the elders and among the flock.

Peter then changed the imagery by saying, *"Shepherd the flock which is among you,"* so there was a real sense of intermingling and mutual belonging. The shepherd doesn't feel like a stranger among the sheep, and the sheep don't feel like strangers among their overseers. These people were connected, in the goodness of God; they belonged to one another. The Greek language puts it differently for it speaks about 'the among you flock' – *to en humin poimnion* – and this emphasises they are mutually placed, not only to be with one another, but there for one another. The flock was to be comfortable in the shepherds' company to show that:

- God ministers to us through you
- We sense the hand of God in your touch
- We hear the voice of God in your speech
- We see the example of the Lord Jesus Christ in your manner

Everything in the shepherds' conduct was sheep-related. At home on the farm, we can walk through a field and the sheep will scatter, but they will automatically come to the shepherd when he walks through. It's simple - they know who the Shepherd is. They know his voice and can sense his movements. Their eyes are rectangular, and have such good peripheral vision they can see behind them without turning their heads. They also have good memories and recognise those who care for them. Spiritually speaking, these are the kind of eyes spiritual shepherds need. It's not something we are born with, but by the grace of God and the help of the Spirit of God spiritual sight can be formed until it not only has sight, but an ability for insight. This is tremendously important in the heart and work of an overseer.

I Exhort

Peter's view of the flock is commendable for he says, *"I exhort."* What a lovely approach! As an apostle, he had been through three years of ministry with the Saviour walking at his side. He had gone through the difficulties of Calvary and had been wonderfully used as the preacher at Pentecost. Now, as he writes, he has the authority of a man who has been called of God. He is Christlike in his appreciation of eternal and sacrificial grace, and has the authority to speak to them about their worship and witness, because he is a well-formed worshipper and fearless witness.

He also speaks with the authority of a married man whose wife accompanied him in the Lord's work (4), and well equipped with spiritual gifts. By the time he addressed the elders in chapter 5, they would be in no doubt that he spoke with authority on each aspect of Christian service. Now he is the well-rounded overseer, shaped for the purpose and authorised by God to write to them. In other words, he lived his own letter. So what would he say, and how would he say it?

He could have said, *"I command you in the name of the Lord"* or *"I demand as an apostle with apostolic authority,"* but he didn't. He could have ordered them, but he spoke in pastoral grace, *"I exhort,"* and the word he used means he was coming alongside to call them. Even by the way he spoke, he drew near to work beside them. It's as if he were saying, "I want to draw near to you, and I want my ministry to have an effect on you. I want you to sense the voice of God in what I'm saying."

How tragic it would have been if God had not been heard! Oh, if this doesn't happen in our ministry there's something seriously missing, but there was nothing missing in Peter's. Along with his word of encouragement, there was his attitude of fellow-involvement: *"I who am a fellow elder."* This was the bondservant speaking. He could have said, *"I exhort you, I who am an apostle of Jesus Christ,"* and who would have questioned it? By divine inspiration, God spoke through His servant as a fellow shepherd, a fellow overseer, a fellow elder. He wasn't above them, nor were they beneath him. He was beside them as an equal. No tiers, only tears!

If you went to a market on a day when sheep were being sold, the men that lean on the ring bidding have only one thing in their minds. They are not talking about a host of other things, they are thinking about sheep. Meet shepherds at their work or in their homes, and it's highly likely they will be talking about sheep. What about us? When as elders we go into each other's company, does the conversation automatically turn to sheep; and sheep, in your homes does the conversation automatically turn to shepherds? That's the way it should be – not in a critical sense, but constructively with the voice of appreciation being heard.

Shepherd the Flock

When God was speaking through Peter about shepherding the flock, he used a word that simply means 'to feed'; so the verse could easily say, "Feed the flock of God." It's an interchangeable word. The Shepherd is expected to feed, he's a feeder; and the flock is entitled to be fed. When we walk and work among the saints of God as shepherds our priority is to feed.

The only time sheep will come to a stranger in a field is when they hear the familiar sound of a bag of feed or smell the attraction of a bale. In one way, it's very easy to feed sheep – you just need to go into the field, scatter some feed and they'll come. It may be different in wintertime. There are times when deep snow means it's a long way down to uncover any grass, and it would be pointless to throw cake or hay into the snow. A space must be cleared where you can spread some feeding, so it's not simply a matter of making it available, it has to be accessible.

That's the work of the overseer, too. He must make the teaching of God's Word accessible as well as available. It has to be something that's enjoyable; not something they have to search for, but something that has been searched out for them. The shepherd has to provide in a way that means the sheep can't miss it, and it has to be the number one priority that he doesn't leave the field without knowing his sheep have been fed. There's a whole range of ministry that is reflected in shepherding and if you were following a shepherd on a farm you would soon discover lots of spiritual parallels. In many ways, we would see things being done that ought to have counterparts in your church.

The New King James version of the Bible quotes Peter as speaking to men who are *"serving as overseers,"* which is clearer than the Revised Version's *"exercising the oversight."* The word *"oversight"* is easily misunderstood and misapplied. Many use it to describe an overseers' meeting or a company of overseers, but the word Peter used – *episkopountes* – isn't an adjective or a noun. It's a verb, so oversight is something that overseers do and applies to overseers overseeing, and to when these particular men are doing what they are. This is similar to what we have in Psalm 23. We are accustomed to saying, *"The LORD is my Shepherd,"* yet the Hebrew word *ra'ah* is a verb and means "The LORD shepherds me." Other examples of this are found in Ezekiel 34 where the same word for shepherd is a verb six times in verse 2 and throughout the chapter.

It seems unlikely that Peter could write about this without thinking of the Lord's conversation with him after His resurrection when He spoke about feeding and tending His sheep. The words can mean very different things for feeding is something that can be done when sheep are together, whereas there are other aspects of shepherding that can't be done collectively.

Tending sheep can include shearing, dipping, dosing, paring sore feet, or helping one that has fallen on to its back. Each of these must be done individually. It's very evident in shearing - as soon as you take the fleece from a sheep, you will likely see it leap in the air. It will normally hoist itself as if it were on springs at the delight at being released from the weight it's been carrying around. That's one effect a shepherd can have by doing one job – but there are other things too.

In a similar way, the flock of God can be fed when the assembly is together and more widely at District conferences and the like, but it's very unlikely that tending will be achieved without personal interaction with the shepherd. There are times when sheep have to be medicated. But there's no point in medicating one and assuming that others will benefit. In our work with one another, the pastoral evidence of grace is the spiritual good that shepherds provide for each one. As assistants of the great Shepherd who has gone above, we need to know what medication each sheep needs. We need to ask, "What is there about its behaviour that I need to understand?" If we don't understand the way of a sheep we will never understand how to medicate it, and that's one of the great ministries of shepherding in the spiritual atmosphere of an assembly.

There are times when a sheep has to be turned upside down and its feet examined because something, such as dried mud or a small stone, has compacted between the cleats of its feet. The sheep will limp around and its walk may be so badly affected it will not lie down. As it moves around, it needs the eye of the shepherd to spot it and deal with its feet, for only then will it walk normally and be able to rest. There's a day coming when God will gather the lame (5) and, by His great shepherding, He will bring Israel back to Himself. He will show them the Man of Calvary, their limping days will be over, and they will walk with Him at last (6).

Sometimes a sheep may fall over on its back and not be able to right itself, especially if its fleece is heavy. The only way to help is to stand the sheep up between your legs and stay there until it recovers. Leaving it too soon to stand on its own can mean it will tumble over again, due to poor blood circulation in its legs. Christians can go through stages of limping too, and we can be in real danger of losing them if we don't attend to their walk at the proper time or spend enough time with them. There are times in our Christian lives when all these shepherding skills are needed in a spiritual sense: the shepherds need to be aware of the opportunity, and the sheep also need to be aware that they can depend on the shepherd providing that ministry.

It was David who said, *"He makes me to lie down in green pastures"* (7). Sheep are not dogs. You can't tell one to sit, and it's impossible to make one lie down. You have to be able to look at sheep and know what will 'cause' them to lie down. This is what David meant. Provide the right conditions and they will lie down. It's one of the wonders of shepherding that the sheep know themselves when to lie down but the shepherd has a lot to do with it. First of all, he has to make sure they're fed and well-watered. Sheep won't lie down if they are still hungry or thirsty; nor will they lie down if there's something wrong with their feet; and thirdly, they won't lie down if there's a predator in the field. The sound or sighting of a fox in a field will keep sheep from lying down. They will circle their lambs, protecting them as best as they can. If they have twins, they can cope, but if she has triplets then one of them is almost guaranteed to go, because she can't protect all three.

Overseers are not superhuman, neither are their sheep, and sometimes they get stretched in how they are to look after this one and that one. The danger is that while looking after one they may just miss the attack that is taking place on another. It's a difficulty that shepherds, both natural and spiritual, have to admit. The opportunity of being everywhere at once is just not possible.

Likewise, You Younger

Peter deals so patiently with these dear men that are doing the shepherding work, and then he urges younger men to submit to them – now there are those who take this to mean he was addressing younger overseers and, if that's what you think of the portion, let me be the last to take it away from you. However, it seems equally likely that he was broadening his appeal and application, just as he did in chapter 3 with *"wives ... husbands ... all of you."* It seems to be by the same widening of his reasoning that a further aspect of submission is presented in chapter 5 – *"The elders ... Likewise you younger ... all of you"* – as widening circles. The elders are like moulds – Gr. *tupos*: types or patterns – for others to emulate. As elders, in more ways than one, he calls for them to be respected, and for everyone in the churches to embrace the opportunity to wear the servant's apron of submission and humility.

In this way, everyone would know that they are important to the shepherds, and the shepherds would know that they are important to the sheep. Peter must have thought about the Lord Jesus Christ giving this example to His disciples in the Upper Room when He laid aside his garments, just as he had laid aside His glory. And now he says *"be clothed with humility"* – be like the Saviour, humble yourselves under the mighty hand of God. He wore the towel for our sakes, and now we hear Peter's appeal to wear the apron for His sake!

The Chief Shepherd

Peter would never forget the day when the Good Shepherd came to his beach looking for fishermen (8), and he left his nets to follow Him. Following wasn't always his strongpoint, and he knew that he had let Him down, but then the Great Shepherd (9) appeared in resurrection and spoke to him about the matter of leadership (10). In marvellous grace he was then enabled to preach in Jerusalem in response to the coming of the Holy Spirit, and how able he was! Quoting freely from Joel's prophecy and from David's psalms, he spoke as a man of God who was immersed in the Word of God and filled by the Spirit of God to speak about the Christ of God (11). At the end of his message, he watched as droves of sheep came forward at the sound of their Shepherd's voice, and they followed Him into the first church planting that ever took place.

The Lord introduced himself as the good Shepherd (12) – the dying One; the writer to the Hebrews introduced Him as the great Shepherd – the risen One; but it was Peter the leader who introduced Him as the Chief Shepherd – the coming One. As we wait for His coming, what a blessing it would be, and what assemblies we would be, if every sheep and every lamb knew that the hand of a shepherd had touched it, ministered to it, assisted it whether in its walk or in its feeding as a demonstration of the pastoral grace of God.

(1) Eph.5:2 (2) 1 Thess.5:12; Heb.13:7,17, 24 (3) Acts 20:28; 1 Thess.5:12 (4) 1 Cor.9:5 (5) Mic.4:6, NIV (6) Zech.12:10 (7) Ps.23:2 (8) Matt.4:18-22 (9) Heb.13:20 (10) Jn 21:15-17 (11) Acts 2 (12) Jn 10:11,14

1 Peter 5:10-12

"But may the God of all grace, who called us to His eternal glory by Christ Jesus, after you have suffered a while, perfect, establish, strengthen, and settle you. To Him be the glory and the dominion forever and ever. Amen. By Silvanus, our faithful brother as I consider him, I have written to you briefly, exhorting and testifying that this is the true grace of God in which you stand" (1 Peter 5:10-12).

10. GRACE REGAINED IN BIBLICAL TRUTHS

God has His own way of showing that He is the source and the supplier. There are different times when He reveals Himself as the "God of," and then says that something is "of God."

As he came to the end of his letter, Peter knew that grace had been well presented, like the recurring movement of a musical overture that comes to the fore, only to recede before rising again to a more rousing finale. But he knew that he wasn't the composer, and that the variations had come from a greater mind than his own. It was in this certainty that he bound them together in unison to ascribe glory to their source in *"the God of all grace"* and to exalt Him as the sharer of *"the true grace of God."* So the character of God comes out in what He does and the glories of His Being are shared with us in such a way that He is glorified in those who own His grace.

Having traced its varied applications in all he has written, it's as if Peter wanted to gather the whole message under one canopy before closing. He had been given the honour of being one of God's penmen, but he knew that while he was the communicator of God's grace, he was not its mediator. This belongs to the One who called him from his boat to cast a greater net for Him, and he knew that all its facets would cause us, like Paul, to speak of it as *"the grace of our Lord Jesus Christ"* (1).

When Paul was closing his second letter to Corinth, in his benediction – *"the grace of the Lord Jesus Christ, and the love of God, and the communion of the Holy Spirit"* (2) - he was thinking about the grace of the One who:

- Gave Himself for us (Galatians 2:20)
- Saved us (Ephesians 2:8)
- Brought us to God (Hebrews 2:10; 1 Peter 3:18)
- Pleads for us before God (Romans 8:34; 1 John 2:1)
- Receives and perfects our worship (1 Peter 2:5)
- Is coming for us (1 Corinthians 15:50,51)

The letter to the Hebrews speaks about the Holy Spirit being *"the Spirit of grace"* (3), so He also fulfils an intermediary role. Just as we are indebted to the Saviour for bringing us to God through His redeeming and reconciling work on the cross, we owe deep gratitude to the Spirit of grace for bringing us to Christ. It is in grace that He:

- Convict us of sin, and of righteousness, and of judgment"
- Guides us into all truth
- Reveals the beauties of Christ to us (John 16:8,13,14)
- Intercedes for us in prayer (Romans 8:27)
- Leads us in our daily walk (Galatians 6:16)
- Leads us in worship and prayer (Philippians 3:3; Ephesians 6:18)

All three Persons put us hand in hand with each other, so that we might enjoy fellowship with Them. It doesn't mean that the Son's saving work caused God's grace to be given to us; it's the other way around: the grace of God the Father caused the saving work of the Lord Jesus to bring His salvation. We look at Him, as John did in chapter 1 of his gospel, and we see Him as *"full of grace."* He is what God is, and the grace of the triune, co-equal God is behind the wealth of grace through which we are saved and kept. Together, They are *"the God of all grace."*

There's no shortage of references to grace in the world. Many speak of "the grace of god", but it's of a god with a small 'g.' It was no different in Peter's day. Idols were everywhere, yet they were incapable of imparting grace, and it's still the same. They have mouths that can't speak, so there are no words of grace; they have eyes that can't see, so there's no look of grace; they have hands that can't handle, so there's no touch of grace; they have feet that can't walk, so there's no companionship of grace (4). Grace has no source outside of the Father, Son and Holy Spirit, and where there is no source there can be no sharing. It cannot be found elsewhere apart from Them; They are the co-equal source and, having exactly the same nature, They are co-equal sharers.

DOCTRINAL GRACE

But Peter wants to take us farther. He wants us to see that, since grace resides in the God of all grace as one united Person, He shares it through one united purpose in *"the true grace of God."* It's the summation of all he has been writing. It's not that we take refuge in His eternal and sacrificial grace in chapter 1 and decide to go no farther. There's more, much more. Like Paul in Galatians 5, where He who supplies the Spirit expects us to begin and continue by the Spirit, with Peter we begin and continue by grace. Before God in worship, before men in witness in the world and in the workplace, before our families in the home, before the assembly in the discharge of spiritual gifts, and before the flock in leadership, grace abounds.

Going into chapter 1 is like entering an archway that has the inscription,

"The God of all grace," and, having seen all its aspects, we emerge from the other side to read its corresponding statement: *"This is the true grace of God."* Peter has been led by the Spirit of God to gather up all that has been highlighted in a way that was, as he calls it, *di oligōn* – through a little while. It hasn't been a major treatise on each aspect of teaching, yet he was in no doubt that they should give believers a greater sense of God. In the accumulation of grace, in the aggregate of teaching, we should discover, not only that grace is revealed, but a greater revelation of God. This brings us to the question: having paused briefly at each stage, have we been brought closer to Him?

Each aspect of teaching unveils His character, and this in itself should give us affection for and appreciation of doctrine. Sometimes, words such as theology and doctrine are treated as the poor relations of our Christian walk, but Peter's mind is that we need to see them as God sees them. They are His 'doctrinal grace'; the presentation and explanation of His kindness to us in Christ. Even in their suffering, the truths of God's grace were to be the strength in which they would actively take their stand.

> "Leave to His sovereign sway to choose and to command;
> So shalt thou, wondering, own that way,
> How wise, how strong His hand.
> Far, far above thy thought, His counsel shall appear,
> When fully He the work hath wrought that caused thy needless fear."
> (Paul Gerhardt)

Perfect, Establish, Strengthen and Settle

It's probably true that the fisherman can be taken away from fishing, but that fishing can't be taken away from the fisherman. Peter knew all about the work of perfecting. In fact, it would be an everyday practice in Galilee. When the Lord moved on from calling him and Andrew, they were at His side when He called James and John who were busy mending their nets. They'd been out fishing and the nets had broken, so they were going through the careful work of tying the loose ends together to make the fishing net intact again. The fisherman's future depends on this; the Greeks called it *katartizō*, and it's the very word Peter has drawn from his own background and used for *"perfect."*

Like fishing nets, damage can be done to the network of Christian character and conduct, so that they become less effective. The work of repair and restoration is just as vital in Christian life, and Peter lets us know that the God of all grace is ready to mend the mesh that the stresses of life have tested beyond breaking point. In a very different line of work, a doctor would have used the same word for resetting a bone, and this also helps us to see the hand of God at work when someone has been hurt. When things go wrong, He will put them right. Whenever you feel the hurt of things that are hard to understand, He will help to reset the situation. Some nets are harder to mend than others, some bones are so fractured it's almost impossible to reset them, and sometime Christians find it difficult to let the Lord restore them by His grace.

He also will establish you. We are not always as spiritually stable as we should be through our own lack of steadfastness. Times set apart for reading and study of God's Word become less until they disappear altogether, times of prayer go, and our whole sense of having a stable relationship with the Lord is lost. It's a self-inflicted wound, but sometimes others can stumble you. The adversary knows how to use this. Paul asked the Galatians, *"You were running well. Who hindered you?"* (6). He also knows how to keep you from getting over it. Scripture says, *"A brother offended is harder to win than a strong city"* (Prov.18:19), and this is very true, but it's equally true that being unforgiving will stop the stabilising process.

The God of all grace is able to establish you. His grace can cure all instability and solidify your relationship with Him, and He can rebuild when needed, but He has to establish us first. He wants to take what He has given you in salvation and build on it in such a way that the former instability will have gone and He is able to do something through you to His glory.

He also wants to strengthen, to empower you by removing whatever weakness has limited your progress, and replace it with divine strength. Each of us knows the things that cripple spiritual progress, and perhaps mediocrity is among the most likely causes. Did you ever think that this could be the biggest danger in churches, too? We can be content with the ordinary when we have a God of unlimited ability who is able to build, develop and expand through us if only we would allow Him.

Another is being content to drift along in the shallows without ever going deeper, happy with an average middle-of-the-road sort of commitment. Daniel's words are as true today as they always were: *"the people who know their God shall be strong, and carry out great exploits"* (7). There's a tendency in our lives for something to creep in and obstruct the perfecting work that God wants to fulfil, something that prevents whatever He wants to build in us. He is able to reach others and touch them through us, yet mediocrity and the possibility of just drifting along will remove the opportunity of the Spirit of God ministering to others in such a way that He not only strengthens you but helps others to be strengthened through you.

Finally, God wants to settle you. You may look back on times when you felt really unsettled, as if the foundation of your Christian life had been shaken. Being settled is the opposite of being unstable, and God wants to replace that unsettled feeling. You will remember that when dear old Jacob was dying, he gathered his twelve boys at his bedside and had something very personal to say to each of them. Here was an old father speaking to his boys for the last time. One thing is certain, none of them would ever forget what was said to him. Starting with the eldest, he said, *"Reuben, you are ... unstable as water"* (8).

If you had been standing at that bedside, can you think of what he would have said to you?God knows that all of us need to be stabilised by a foundation, and that spiritual service is impossible without one. Even the portable structure of the tabernacle had one in the form of its "sockets." They were called *'eden*, which can also mean "foundation" (9). They are related to *'adōn* (lord), and *Adonāi*, such as in Psalm 8:1 – *"O LORD, our Lord [Yahweh'Adonēnū] how excellent is Your name in all the earth!"* So the tabernacle stood in sockets that announced His lordship. Later, the temple had its foundations of *"large stones, costly stones, and hewn stones"* (10), so that God's dwelling place on earth might reflect what He has done in heaven.

Of it, He says, *"Behold, I lay in Zion a stone for a foundation, a tried stone, a precious corner stone, a sure foundation."* He was speaking of His exalted Son, and risen Victor of the cross: well proven, infinitely precious, and eternally sure. His own description of Christ is that He is a *"sure foundation,"* which in Hebrew is *musād mussād*. In Psalm 45:2, He is seen as *yāpheyāphiythā*, "fair fair" or "beautiful beautiful," and

130

both duplications mean He is beyond description. As Son, and Stone, He is greater, costlier and more tested than any other, and it's only on Him that God can *"perfect, establish, strengthen, and settle you."*

It's for this reason that one aspect of His true grace is to lay a sure foundation for our lives of service, and to make it possible the Son became identified with His Father making Him perfect. For our sakes He experienced *katartizō* when God "prepared" a body for Him, He was prepared for suffering, and it was this that allowed *"the grace of God"* to appear (11). In the experience of believers, God perfects them through suffering. The wonderful truth is that Christ's perfect network of attributes is made known to us through the teaching of Scripture, and it's this that allowed John to write, *"He who abides in the doctrine of Christ has both the Father and the Son"* (12). It takes the truth that is in Jesus (13) to let us know Him and enjoy everything that belongs to the true grace of God.

Perfected

There is something else to enjoy. The one whom God made perfect for suffering also knew what it was to be *"made perfect"* (RV) through suffering (14). Unlike Aaron, who became high priest and offered many sacrifices for others and himself, Jesus offered one sacrifice for sins forever (15) – for others, and not Himself – and was *"perfected"* (16).

The thought, this time, is very different. Instead of *katartizō*, the word is now *teleiōtheis*, which means He became the completer of His Father's will. As finisher of the work that had been given Him to do, He entered into the gain of His cross as the author, the cause, of eternal salvation. He also became equipped as High Priest, having been *"perfected forever"* (17).

So, He is the means of our salvation; we have been *"perfected forever"* and set apart in holiness (18). He also is the means of our service. He came as the perfect Man and, having fulfilled His Father's will as sin-bearer, went Home as the perfected Man. As for believers, He has brought us into His Father's will, and we are going Home perfected forever.

As we listen to these closing verses of Peter's letter, what is our response as he says, *"May the God of all Grace, who called us to His eternal glory in Christ Jesus ... perfect ... you."*? Will you let him perfect you? Do you know of areas in your life where He needs to perfect you? Could you actually sit down and identify what He sees that others may not see? They might think you are doing fine, but we know there are times when, under the eyesight of God, something is being seen that only He and we know about. He wants to perfect us, that in our maturing He may see integrity, quality and stability and the removal of frailty, impurity, mediocrity and instability.

Will we let Him remove them?

Of course, He may ask to walk through each of Peter's five chapters with you and ask you to read it as He were at your side. To settle you, He may want to spend some time with you, just to have a talk about each one.

Will you let Him:

- Restore to you the joy of His salvation in chapter 1?
- Refresh your worship and witness in chapter 2?
- Renew your marriage and revive your desire for holiness in chapter 3?
- Reignite the flame of usefulness in your gift in chapter 4?
- Recover your zeal to lead or be led in chapter 5?

The God of all grace is asking you to take your stand and, as you pause with Him chapter by chapter, He will give you the grace to keep standing in the true grace of God till Jesus comes.

> "Shall we, dare we disappoint Him? Brethren, let us rise!
> He who died for us is watching from the skies."
> (Alice J. Janvrin)

(1) 2 Cor.8:9 (2) 2 Cor.13:14 (3) Heb.10:29 (4) Ps.115:5-7 (5) Gal.3:3-5 (6) Gal.5:7, ESV (7) Dan.11:32 (8) Gen.49:3,4 (9) Job 38:6 (10) 1 Kin.5:17 (11) Tit.2:11 (12) 2 Jn 9 (13) Eph.4:21 (14) Heb.5:8,9 (15) Heb.7:27; 10:12 (16) Heb.5:9 (17) Heb.7:28 (18) Heb.10:14

2 Corinthians 8:9

"*For you know the grace of our Lord Jesus Christ, that though He was rich, yet for your sakes He became poor, that you through His poverty might become rich*" (2 Corinthians 8:9).

11. GRACE RE-EMPHASISED IN PAUL'S LETTERS

Do you ever look at a verse in your Bible and ask it a question? For instance, why is God saying this right here when the same verse would seem so apt in many other places? Could it not have been appropriately slotted into Peter's letter alongside one of his many references to grace? Let's imagine we had been absorbing what he said about God's 'eternal grace' in chapter 1, and thinking of what this meant to the Saviour in His condescension. Would we have been surprised if he then went on to say, *"For you know the grace of our Lord Jesus Christ, that though He was rich, yet for your sakes He became poor, that you through His poverty might become rich"*?

Had we been thinking of 'sacrificial grace' and the value of the Lord Jesus Christ offering Himself to God for His satisfaction as well as ours, would Paul's words not have been a very fitting addition? When the Holy Spirit led us and put our hands into the hands of Christ to know Him as our Saviour, right at that moment God could have said, *"You know the grace of our Lord Jesus Christ."*

The same question could be asked as we read on and apply it to thoughts of experimental grace that causes us to worship God and witness to others. Would it not have relevance to us as we experience 'marital grace' in our home lives? Then He enriches us again through the variegated grace of spiritual gifts, and we seek to fill the place for which He has fitted us. At that point too, He says, "You know." The whole way through to what we have considered of 'pastoral grace' and 'doctrinal grace,' would it have felt out of place if these words about the Lord's enriching grace were attached?

No, at any one of these points we probably would feel the impact of the Spirit of God as He whispers, "You know ... you know." Peter's letter is so Christ-centred, but these words don't belong here; God has set them in 2 Corinthians 8:9, so we have to decide why they are there and not in 1 Peter with all the accumulated reference to the wonders of God's grace.

Paul tells us why it's here. It's because the Macedonians were an outstanding example of giving and he was giving the church in Corinth a lesson on generosity based on the dear ones in the churches in Berea, Philippi and Thessalonica. He was using them as a model, but wanted to raise Corinth's sights even higher to the greatest Giver of all by saying, *"For you know the grace of our Lord Jesus Christ, that though He was rich, yet for your sakes He became poor, that you through His poverty might become rich."* It was said in the context of selfless surrender that was for the good of others, and there is no greater example of this than the Saviour Himself. There are many who give of themselves, but only One who gave Himself! He went out bearing the cross for Himself, knowing that it would bear Him, and that on it He would bear our sins in His own body. It's also true that there have been many gracious men and women, but only He is "Grace."

When God says, *"You know the grace of our Lord Jesus Christ,"* He expects us to breathe in the value of what He has breathed out. These are His words about His Son who is "The grace" – co-equal with the God of all grace of 1 Peter 5:10. As co-equal, He also is co-eternal, and this is included in the words *"though He was rich."* The word "was" sounds very ordinary, but God is so exact He uses two different words to convey what He means. One means "always was", and the other means "became." The Son of God is eternally rich, but became temporarily poor. The difference is set out in John 1. In verses 1, 2 and 4, the word "was" is the same six times. It is *ēn*, which belongs to the word *eimi*. When we read of the Lord being the "I AM", the words are *egō eimi*, which means He eternally was, is, and will be. He is the eternal Word, the eternal light, and the eternal life.

The striking thing about John is that He knew when to use this word, and he knew when not to use it. However, when he said, *"without Him nothing was made that was made,"* he used a different word. This time he twice uses *egeneto*, which means it became or it happened. So there's a hugely important distinction between the two words. God is very careful in His use of words and He never leaves His writers with loose grammar.

His Poverty

If you are already thinking that Paul used the first word, you are absolutely right. By saying, *"He was rich,"* he meant eternally rich, the riches of the eternal I AM. But He became poor, not simply in a financial way, but in His whole lifestyle that brought the limitations of hunger, thirst, tiredness and weakness. And He did this *"for your sakes."* His poverty in becoming our substitute has brought us the riches of His substitutionary work. How humbling it is that this purpose was in the counsels of Deity even before creation, and overwhelming to think that the place of substitution was marked out as it was being created. As Abraham and Isaac made their way to Moriah, the Maker watched and knew they were bound for the place where He would give His life as a ransom for many (1). Yes, God will provide the lamb (2), and He did it at Calvary in the Lamb slain from the foundation of the world (3).

Brothers and sisters, you know the grace of our Lord Jesus Christ. He gave Himself sacrificially, substitutionally and sovereignly in the sovereignty of God. Does that not move you? Does it not make you bow at your Saviour's feet to thank Him for thinking you were worth it? He is not only wealthy, He is worthy, yet through His poverty He took your unworthiness to transform you. God designed you and took that old clay jar, broke you at your Saviour's feet, and turned you into a vessel of mercy prepared beforehand for glory (4). For your sake He became poor.

El Shaddai the Mighty One was crucified in weakness. God the eternal was confined in six hours of absolute agony and misery, God the all-knowing wondering why the Father had forsaken Him; yet knowing, at the same time, it was that He might never forsake us. He laid aside His glory that He might bring us to glory. These are contrasts that He built into his life for our sakes. He became poor, but how do you define the poverty of Christ? The Lord used the same word about Lazarus: "*a certain beggar*" (5), which means He became beggarly poor. But did he mean financially? Was it only by asking the spies to show Him a penny (6) that He demonstrated His poverty? No, the poverty of Christ has nothing to do with being financial, or our riches in Him would be financial. This is no prosperity gospel, other than that he makes your soul prosper not your pocket.

Is there not something far richer about the Lord Jesus to be experienced than financial? Is the answer not that, just as His poverty was identified with His humanity partaking of our humanity, so our riches belong to being linked with the riches of his divinity? We are partakers of the divine nature (7). He became a partaker of flesh and blood (8), and was made in the likeness of sinful flesh (9). He had the resemblance, but was never an identical. He partook of our humanity, but not our depravity. The ingredient of sin was missing, yet it was in becoming Man that He became poor.

Our Riches

In the north of Burma, it's common to see eggs in the collection box, cabbages and bananas laid on the floor beside it, and rice poured into a separate basket. This is how they fulfil 1 Corinthians 16:2 – *"On the first day of the week let each one of you lay something aside, storing up as he may prosper."* They know how to give, as the Macedonians did, and we could borrow Paul's words to describe them: *"sorrowful, yet always rejoicing; as poor, yet making many rich; as having nothing, and yet possessing all things."* Do we ever wonder if we might be in danger of possessing all things materially, yet having nothing spiritually?

Once again, we hear the words, *"He became poor, that you through His poverty might become rich."* He never had to become rich, but He did have to become poor. We are just the opposite. We didn't have to become poor, but we did need to become rich. He saw us in our poverty and gave up His riches to sacrifice Himself to bring us to God and into His riches. But what are they?

- The riches of His **goodness** speak of what He does. He leads sinners to repentance. In His goodness, He brings us out of the poverty of sin, its guilt and sorrow, into the riches of His forgiveness, peace and hope. Even repentance itself is a blessing for, even though it is the result of godly sorrow, it brings us into the joy of salvation and never brings regret (10).

- The riches of His **grace** speak of what He gives. He causes us to discover the good pleasure of His will by which He grants redemption through his blood with the forgiveness of sins to all who are chosen in Christ before the foundation of the world, that we should be holy and without blemish before Him in love (11).
- The riches of His **glory** speak of who He is. He shares the splendour of His own Being with our redeemed beings through the inner power of His Spirit and presence of Christ. Isn't that just like God? What grace to say He would grant you according to the riches of His glory, so that we might know what it is to be moved by His might and power through His Spirit in the inner man!

Having already known the riches of His goodness that prepare us for salvation, and the riches of His grace that provide us with salvation, God continues to share the riches of His glory so that He might be prominent in us after salvation. Only through the riches of His own glory can we enjoy the blessing of sharing His attributes – His might, His love, and every aspect of His likeness (12).

The author G.F. Dempster is known to have said, "In all Christians, Christ is present; in some Christians, He is prominent; but in very few Christians, Christ is preeminent. God's purpose is that *"in all things He may have the preeminence"* (13), and those who long for the riches of His glory and to be "filled with all the fulness of God" share His desire. We bring ourselves to Him like small containers before a much larger vessel. It's *of* His fulness we have all received (14), not *all* His fulness! The Immeasurable is filling the measurable:

- According to the good pleasure of His will
- According to the riches of His grace
- According to the riches of His glory (15)

The Infinite is filling the finite. We have no lack for He gives abundant life, abundant grace, abundant joy, abundant mercy, and to have the Holy Spirit abundantly (16).

The wonder of God manifested in the flesh is that He is perfect in body, soul and spirit. Well might we say of Him, as Job said of God, "He is unique, and who can make Him change? And whatever His soul desires, that He does" (17). He is completely at one with Himself, so that His character and conduct are one, His intentions and actions are one. He is unchangeable. He stands alone. No matter how godly we may become this will never be said of us, yet we need the riches of His glory before our behaviour can match our beliefs. One way of seeing this is in how we deal with one another. Paul pleaded with the disagreeable Corinthians "by the meekness and gentleness of Christ" (18), and the Manhood of Christ was being reflected in him.

When he wrote to the churches in Galatia, he urged them to act in the same way toward any who had been caught off guard and had sinned. Somewhere, someone may have been waiting to be restored – and, here again, Paul uses the fisherman's word that Peter used, *katartizō*, mend the broken net. No fisherman would let untrained hands near his damaged net, and it's better that no untrained hands ever attempt to "restore" those who have slipped up and lapsed into sin. This is why Paul's three conditions are so vital:

- You who are spiritual – the great need is for mature servants of God who are Spirit-filled and Spirit-led. They will be Word-based, and prayerfully caring in their approach.
- Restore – they must not be heavy-handed or ham-fisted. No net will be improved by clumsy handling; neither will any damaged child of God. Being well-meaning or well-intentioned isn't enough. We

need to be, as Joshua and Caleb said under different circumstances, *"well able to overcome"* (19).

- · A spirit of gentleness – the Lord was masterly at this, and was the essence of being *"well able to overcome."* He is meek and lowly in heart (20), and He knew how to speak a word in season to him who is weary (21). The way He won us is the way we have to win others, with soft words tenderly spoken (22). What a lesson for us! How easy to trip ourselves up just by a wrong word and impulsive reactions. We can be impatient, even when trying not to, but we will never hear impatient words from Him.

If only our tongues didn't work as fast as our minds! A thought gets sparked and immediately it ignites the tongue that's a flame of fire (23) and out it goes, too quickly to be caught and brought back. It's gone, and that flame may do burning damage in someone's mind that they might never forget. But how do we get a spirit of gentleness? It comes from the riches of His glory, as we let the nature of Christ speak through us. Galatians 6 opens with the need for "a spirit" that is right for the job, and it ends with the only way to get it: *"Brethren, the grace of the Lord Jesus Christ be with your spirit."*

So the end of the chapter answers its opening. It tells us how God meets our need before we can meet the other person's need. Those who enjoy fellowship with God are best prepared to help someone's restoration to fellowship with Him. How does such a brother or sister feel welcome unless there's a spirit of meekness being shown? But how can it be shown unless we have been in the presence of God and He has shown it to us? If He has, then both parties will see the grace of the Lord Jesus Christ in each other. What a fitting time to hear the echo of Paul's words, "You know ..."!

As we gather up something of Paul's appreciation of God's grace, we hear his comments on other aspects of God's character. The foolishness of God is wiser than men, and the weakness of God is stronger than men (24). Well might he say these things, for he also wrote that "the message of the cross is foolishness to those who are perishing, but to us who are being saved it is the power of God" (25). He also wrote, "He was crucified in weakness, yet He lives by the power of God" (26). Finally, we read these outstanding words again, "You know the grace of our Lord Jesus Christ, that though He was rich, yet for your sakes He became poor, that you through His poverty might become rich," and it's as if we hear the apostle reply, 'And the poverty of Christ is richer than men!' With thankful hearts, we also reply, "We know!"

(1) Matt.20:28 (2) Gen.22:8 (3) Rev.13:8 (4) Rom.9:23 (5) Lk.16:20 (6) Lk.20:24 (7) 2 Pet.1:4 (8) Heb.2:14 (9) Rom.8:3 (10) Rom.2:4; 2 Cor.7:10 (11) Eph.1:4-7 (12) Eph.3:16-19 (13) Col.1:18 (14) Jn 1:16 (15) Eph.1:5,7; 3:16 (16) Jn 10:10; Rom.5:17; 2 Cor.8:2; 1 Pet.1:3; Tit.3:6 (17) Job 23:13 (18) 2 Cor.10:1 (19) Num.13:30 (20) Matt.11:29 (21) Isa.50:4 (22) Prov.15:1 (23) Jas.3:6 (24) 1 Cor.1:25 (25) 1 Cor.1:18 (26) 2 Cor.13:4

* * *

THE GOD OF SMALL THINGS
(Psalm 24:1; Micah 5:2; Mark 3:9; 1 Corinthians 1:27-29)

"Of all the galaxies that fill
The limitless expanse of space,
God chose this little place called Earth
And here revealed the matchless worth
Of One so full of truth and grace.

Of all the towns in Israel spread,
Whose fame was never held in doubt,
He chose Ephrathah's House of Bread
To birth the One whose coming forth
Was known by Him from going out.

Of all the ships that plied the coast
And braved the Galilean Sea,
He chose a little boat as host
To wait on Him, to bear the cost,
And serve its Guest compliantly.

So, instantly it left the fleet
Of other ships of high degree,
That it might bow beneath His feet
And, like disciples, steadfastly
Be yielded to His Captaincy.

How can we glory – of this world,
And lowlier far than Galilee?
He calls us, foolish, weak and base,
Unknown and nothing, yet by grace
He lifts us up to fill the place

Of wisdom, strength, and known by Him.
No longer least, no longer lost,
For in His cross He paid the cost,
That in His presence now we boast
And praise His Name eternally."

About the Publisher

Hayes Press (hayespress.org) is a registered charity in the United Kingdom, whose primary mission is to disseminate the Word of God. It is one of the largest distributors of gospel tracts and leaflets in the United Kingdom, with over 100 titles and many thousands dispatched annually. In addition to paperbacks and eBooks, Hayes Press also publishes Golden Bells, a popular daily Bible reading calendar. If you would like to contact Hayes Press, please eMail: info@hayespress.org

About the Author

Andy was born in Glasgow, Scotland, He came to know the Lord in 1954, and was baptized in 1958. He is married to Anna, and he lives in Kilmacolm, Scotland. They have two daughters and one son. He entered into full-time service in 1976 with the churches of God (www.churchesofgod.info). He has engaged in an itinerant ministry in western countries and has been privileged to serve the Lord in India and Myanmar (formerly Burma).

Also by Andy McIlree

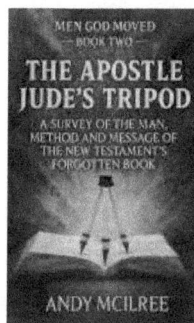

The Apostle Jude's Tripod

As Jude wrote his little book, it's as if he did so with the mindset of a surveyor, scanning the worrying spiritual landscape in front of him - 19 times in his short letter, Jude moves his surveyor's 'tripod' of threes to drive his point home. In addition to exploring each of these, Bible teacher Andy McIlree unpacks each verse across seven key themes of Salutation, Salvation, Contention, Condemnation, Revelation, Benediction and Doxology.

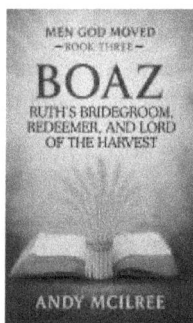

Boaz, Ruth's Bridegroom, Redeemer and Lord of the Harvest

Andy explores the depths of this wonderful Old Testament book of Ruth, and in particular how Boaz is a picture of the Lord Jesus as our Kinsman-redeemer, Bridegroom and the Lord of the Harvest. "The account of Ruth's arrival on the pages of God's Word is an interweaving of His grace, His call and His purpose. So, during Israel's dull days, she is like a colourful butterfly emerging from a very drab chrysalis. There is no shallow end to the story of Ruth, as depths of despair at the beginning lead on to deepening delight, which causes us to exclaim, "Oh, the depth of the riches both of the wisdom and knowledge of God! How unsearchable are His judgments and His ways past finding out!"

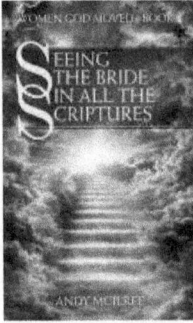

Seeing the Bride in All the Scriptures

Andy explores how some women in the Bible are used by God to paint a beautiful picture of the relationship between the Jesus the Bridegroom and His bride, the Church. Andy begins in Genesis and continue in the Books of the Law, before flowing on through the Psalms and the Prophets - and on the way looks at the types and shadows present in Eve, Rebekah, Israel, the Shulamite of the Song of Songs, Ruth and more. Not only does this book emphasise the importance of women in God's purposes, but it draws us in to better enjoy the love, protection and communion of our Saviour, our Beloved.

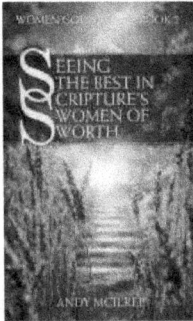

Seeing the Best in Scripture's Women of Worth

Andy looks at some of the doors that God may open for His women: Deborah: Leading (Judg.4:8,9; 5:15) Ruth: Subjecting (Ruth 3:1-7) Abigail: Advising (1 Sam.25:23-31) Shallum's daughters: Building (Neh.3:12) Phoebe: Protecting (Rom.16:1,2) Tryphena & Tryphosa: Labouring (Rom.16:12) Euodia & Syntyche: Witnessing (Phil.4:2,3) These seven examples combine to show what God thinks of His women. They are Women of His worth, Women of His Word, and Women of His Work, and consecrated women are all three!

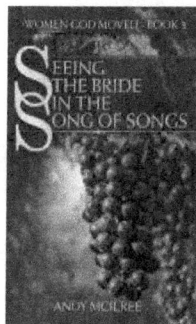

Seeing the Bride in the Song of Songs

Andy explores the often neglected Song of Songs in this devotional commentary. Some question whether it should be in the Bible at all, while many have struggled to understand the purpose of its poetic imagery. Andy invites us to allow its language to first of all lift our thoughts to see God being exalted in His relationship with His people, Israel; these eight chapters display the supremacy of God, clothed in His fervency and intimacy – and even under the Law His working with His people had much grace blended with it. Then, on another level, His Spirit can exalt His Son as we draw lessons that relate to our discipleship walk with Him, and experience "the exceeding riches of His grace in his kindness toward us in Christ."

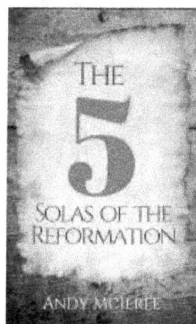

The Five Solas of the Reformation

Five centuries after Luther nailed his Ninety-five Theses to the door of a Catholic church, is there still a need for reformation? Yes, the Reformers' 'Five Solas' - Scripture Alone, Christ Alone, Grace Alone, Faith Alone, the Glory of God Alone - should be engraved on all our hearts, and the need could hardly be greater for them to be nailed to the doors of today's shallow churches today that are in danger of "being destroyed for lack of knowledge" (Hosea 4:6).

149